John Cotton

Revised Edition

Twayne's United States Authors Series

Pattie Cowell, Editor

Colorado State University

TUSAS 80

St. Botolph's Church, Boston, from an 1856 engraving.

John Cotton

Revised Edition

By Everett Emerson

University of North Carolina at Chapel Hill

Twayne Publishers
A Division of G.K. Hall & Co. • *Boston*

John Cotton, Revised Edition
Everett Emerson

First edition copyright 1965 by Twayne Publishers.
Revised edition copyright 1990 by G.K. Hall & Co.
All rights reserved.
Published by Twayne Publishers
A division of G.K. Hall & Co.
70 Lincoln Street
Boston, Massachusetts 02111

Copyediting supervised by Barbara Sutton.
Book production by Nancy Priest.
Book design by Barbara Anderson.
Typeset in 11 pt. Garamond
by Compositors Corporation, Cedar Rapids, Iowa.

First published 1990.
10 9 8 7 6 5 4 3 2 1

The paper used in this publication meets the minimum requirements
of American National Standard for Information Sciences—Permanence
of Paper for Printed Library Materials, ANSI Z39.48-1984. ⊚

Printed and bound in the United States of America.

Library of Congress Cataloging-in-Publication Data

Emerson, Everett H., 1925–
    John Cotton / by Everett Emerson. — Rev. ed.
        p.   cm. — (Twayne's United States authors series ; TUSAS 80)
    Includes bibliographical references and index.
    ISBN 0-8057-7615-X
    1. Cotton, John, 1584–1652.   I. Title.   II. Series.
BX7260.C79E5   1990
285.8′092—dc20   90-37905
                                                              CIP

The picture of St. Botolphs Church, John Cotton's church in Boston,
Lincolnshire, is reproduced from an engraving in Pishey Thompson,
The History and Antiquities of Boston (London: Longman, 1856).

To the memory of
Ann Stanford and Karl Keller,
lovers of poetry, even
Puritan poetry

Contents

About the Author   ix
Preface   xi
Chronology   xiii

Chapter One
The Man and His Age   1

Chapter Two
Pleader for Purity: The Puritan Writings   5

Chapter Three
The Means of Grace: The English Sermons   13

Chapter Four
Champion of the New England Way:
The Congregational Writings   35

Chapter Five
The Means of Grace: The American Sermons   63

Chapter Six
Defender of the Faith: The Theological
Writings   80

Chapter Seven
Spokesman for Organicism: The Controversy
with Roger Williams   103

Chapter Eight
Moses and Aaron Kiss Each Other:
The Political Writings   110

Chapter Nine
Tamer of Impious Sentiments: The Verses   119

Chapter Ten
John Cotton's Significance and Contribution
to American Literature   123

Notes and References   127
Selected Bibliography   138
Index   147

About the Author

Everett Emerson, professor of English and American studies at the University of North Carolina at Chapel Hill, is author or editor of seven books, the first of which was the earlier version of *John Cotton*. He served for twenty years as editor of the journal *Early American Literature* and was the founder of the Mark Twain Circle of America. He has taught in Massachusetts, New York, Pennsylvania, Virginia, Florida, Louisiana, and California, as well as North Carolina.

Preface

The opportunity to revise one's book twenty-five years after its original publication is surely enormously appealing to an author who recognizes how much more knowledge and understanding can be brought to his subject at the later date. What follows is a completely revised study, the result of an effort to accommodate both my own need to understand John Cotton more clearly and the remarkable outpouring of scholarship in the past twenty-five years that has touched the first-generation American Puritan leader.

A few explanations—not apologies: (a) This book is not now and never has been a biography but an attempt to provide a contextual reading of all of Cotton's publications, including some that have only recently appeared. Cotton's life and writings are not wholly separable, and therefore some biographical information is provided. (b) Because Cotton's writings are unavailable to most readers, I have felt obliged to quote much more than if I were dealing with, say, John Updike or Flannery O'Connor. (c) Because my organization is topical, some overlap (but I think not repetition) between chapters has proved necessary. (d) Because a substantial amount of Cotton's writings deal with theology and because some of the major concerns of his life were theological issues, especially in the Antinomian Controversy, there is no way that theology can be neglected in a study of John Cotton.

In 1963 I undertook the task of preparing *John Cotton*, my first book, because I was invited to. My doctoral dissertation was on another early American Puritan, Thomas Hooker, who then engaged me more than Cotton, and despite my best efforts, I did not warm to my subject. My studies had given me a sense of Cotton's English Puritan background, for I was preparing the book that appeared in 1968, *English Puritanism from John Hooper to John Milton*, and I saw ways to use this knowledge, as well as my familiarity with contemporaries of Cotton, such as Thomas Shepard and, of course, Hooker. What I lacked, despite the availability of Larzer Ziff's valuable *The Career of John Cotton*, was a sufficient sense of Cotton's intellectual milieu, with such concerns as his interest in biblical prophecy, millennialism, and spirituality. Cotton was to me a strange and remote figure (his remoteness was a theme of the first edition); I recognized his historical importance but found it hard to grasp fully the quality of the man.

I have now come to a deeper appreciation for both the man and his greatness. John Cotton is the central figure in Theodore Dwight Bozeman's big book *To Live Ancient Lives: The Primitivist Dimension in Puritanism* (1988). Andrew Delbanco's *The Puritan Ordeal* (1989) is a celebration of Cotton as a heroic figure who resisted the disastrous direction that early American Puritanism took. I have looked hard at the early years of Puritanism in my collection *Letters from New England: The Massachusetts Bay Colony, 1629–1638* (1976); and I had the opportunity to take a broader view in preparing my *Puritanism in America, 1620–1750* (1977). As editor of the journal *Early American Literature* I have published two splendid, award-winning essays, one by Teresa Toulouse and the other by Eugenia DeLamotte, that explain some of the subtleties of Cotton's rhetoric of preaching. That is only the tip of a very big iceberg. We have come a long way.

This version of my study pictures Cotton as a far more attractive figure than I found him back in the sixties. He had been a whipping boy for Perry Miller—with whom I had studied, to my enormous profit—and Miller was partly responsible for my earlier perspectives. But mostly that less attractive portrayal arose from my own blindness. The process of improvement began for me with the eye-opening studies of my friends Jesper Rosenmeier and Sacvan Bercovitch. (Miller himself admitted to the former his major mistake about typology: "So I was WRONG, was I?") I am grateful to all who have enlightened me. We shall be further enlightened by Sargent Bush's forthcoming edition of Cotton's correspondence. I thank him for the information he has shared with me. I am grateful to all who have shed light and more light on Cotton, including my eminent colleague and friend Philip F. Gura, and I am thankful that I have access to the riches of the libraries of my university and to the libraries that have served me through interlibrary borrowing.

The portrait used as the frontispiece for the 1965 version of this book proved not to be Cotton. Another portrait, at the Connecticut Historical Society (reproduced in *Letters from New England*), has proved to be inauthentic as well. We shall have to rely on the verbal portraits of his early biographers, Samuel Whiting and John Norton.

Everett Emerson

University of North Carolina at Chapel Hill

Chronology

1584   John Cotton, son of Roland Cotton, lawyer, born in December in Derby, England.

1593–1597   Attends Derby Grammar School.

1597   Matriculates as a sizar at Trinity College, Cambridge University.

1602   Commences bachelor of arts.

1603   Is made fellow of Emmanuel College, Cambridge, a Puritan institution.

1606   Commences master of arts.

1608–1612   Serves, at various times, as head lecturer, dean, and catechist at Emmanuel College.

1609   Attracts attention by preaching funeral sermon for Dr. Robert Some. Experiences religious conversion from preaching of Richard Sibbes.

1610   Is ordained to the priesthood.

ca. 1611   Preaches university sermon that converts John Preston.

1612   Is made vicar of St. Botolph's Church, Boston, Lincolnshire.

1613   Commences bachelor of divinity. Teaches Cambridge students and students from the Continent who have come to live with him, this year and hereafter. Marries Elizabeth Horrocks. Earns annual salary of one hundred pounds.

1615   Establishes "congregational" system within his parish.

1621   St. Botolph's stained glass is destroyed.

1630   Preaches sermon at Southampton to departing members of the Massachusetts Bay Colony.

1631   Elizabeth Horrocks Cotton dies, childless.

1632   Goes into hiding to prevent being summoned to appear before church authorities; is remarried to a widow, Sarah Hawkridge Story.

1633   Resigns from St. Botolph's Church vicarship. Leaves with family for America. First son, Seaborn, is born on voyage. Is chosen teacher of the Boston, Massachusetts, church.

1635   First daughter, Sarah, born.

1636   Is appointed to committee to prepare a draft of laws for the colony.

1636–1637   Roger Williams leaves Massachusetts Bay Colony.

1637   Synod condemns antinomianism. Cotton is appointed to first board of overseers of Harvard College. Daughter Elizabeth born.

1638   Anne Hutchinson is excommunicated.

1640   *The Whole Book of Psalmes* published. John Cotton, Jr., born.

1642   Is invited to England to attend Westminster Assembly but does not go. Daughter Mariah born (she later marries Increase Mather and gives birth to Cotton Mather). Again appointed Harvard overseer.

1643   Serves as joint moderator of conference condemning Presbyterianism. Son Rowland born.

1644   *The Keyes of the Kingdom of Heaven, Mr. Cottons Letter Examined and Answered*, and *The Bloudy Tenent of Persecution* published.

1646–1648   Cambridge Synod.

1647   *The Bloudy Tenent, Washed* and *A Reply to Mr. Williams His Examination* published.

1649   Daughter Sarah and son Rowland die.

1651   Seaborn Cotton graduates from Harvard.

1652   John Cotton dies 23 December in Boston.

Chapter One
The Man and His Age

American culture as traditionally conceived began in New England; the New England contribution to American life and culture continues to be examined by historians, students of literature and religion, sociologists, and political scientists, among others—and by people curious about that peculiar and fascinating phenomenon known as Puritanism. For those who would know New England Puritanism, John Cotton (1584–1652) is a highly important figure. The chief spokesman for what became known as the New England Way, Cotton touched many aspects of early New England life. He was a religious teacher, a lawgiver, a defender of New England ideals, and a historian. He played many roles, for he considered the life of his community as an organic whole. He left a substantial body of writing, forty works, many of continuing interest, though today they require attention to their context to be understood.

Cotton was a clergyman, and for the Puritan minister the most important task was preaching the Word. Many contemporaries considered him the greatest preacher in New England. Cotton Mather quoted John Cotton's colleague in the ministry at his church in Boston, John Wilson, as saying of him: "Mr. Cotton preaches with such authority, demonstration, and life that, methinks, when he preaches out of any prophet or apostle I hear not him; I hear that very prophet and apostle. Yea, I hear the Lord Jesus Christ speaking in my heart."[1] Cotton's sermons compose nineteen volumes of his published works, though some volumes contain only a single sermon. Some are topical, dealing with events of international importance. Most combine scriptural commentary with exhortations, warnings, and consolations; but even these often reveal a sense of time and place. All reveal a man of mildness and profound piety who was dedicated to the creation of a new Israel in America, a society like the one of Old Testament times, wherein church and state would work together cooperatively. I call this concept organicism.

In old England and New, John Cotton was a leading Puritan minister. Before he came to America at the age of forty-nine, Cotton was associated in England with the greatest Puritan preachers of his day. He had heard William Perkins—"Painful" Perkins he was called, because of his diligence and precision—preach at Cambridge, where the influential Richard Sibbes's sermons later converted Cotton. He had studied with another influential Puritan intellectual, Laurence Chaderton, head of Emmanuel College, which served as a model for Harvard College in the New World. He had written a prefatory epistle for an important collection of sermons by another celebrated Puritan, Arthur Hildersam. He was himself responsible for the conversion of the great John Preston. He had sought counsel from the Puritan patriarch John Dod. He was a friend of the English Independent Thomas Goodwin. Samuel Clarke saw to it that Norton's life of Cotton was reprinted in 1662 in *A Collection of the Lives of Ten Eminent Divines*; here he was listed with more of the great ones, among them William Gouge, Thomas Gataker, and Robert Harris.

Till recently, most modern readers of Cotton have expressed great disappointment with his sermons. The father of modern studies of colonial American literature, Moses Colt Tyler, finds no real merit in them. A more recent student of early American sermons, Babette Levy, rates them much below those of Thomas Hooker and Thomas Shepard. Tyler's and Levy's reactions have been typical. It remained for Larzer Ziff, Cotton's biographer, to see that precisely because Cotton is "immured in the seventeenth century" his works "offer us meaningful contact with the shaping past." To study Cotton is to understand the past; his sermons have a "conscious appropriateness to the moment in history."[2] Even more recently, two young scholars—Teresa Toulouse and Eugenia DeLamotte—have shown how Cotton the preacher directed his audience's attention to the figurative language and the imagery of biblical texts in a way that had not been appreciated. We are still learning about John Cotton.

Seven of Cotton's works are expositions or defenses of the New England Way, which Cotton was the first to call congregationalism. More than his sermons, or more at least than most of them, these works provide an insight into the nature of his American experience. Cotton and many of his fellow colonists considered their venture a great witness both to England and to the rest of the world they knew. Though he settled in Massachusetts, Cotton hoped through the force of example and through the persuasiveness of his pen to be able to establish the New England Way in the land he had left.

One of the reasons for Cotton's eminence was his great learning, the result of an extended stay at the University of Cambridge. He was one of two New Englanders of the first generation to hold the bachelor of divinity degree, which required seven years of study beyond the master of arts, which was at that time achieved after three years of residence beyond the bachelor of arts. The Christian humanism that characterizes this education suggests how much Cotton's world differed from our own. At Cambridge, Cotton studied logic, rhetoric, ethics, theology, Latin, Greek, Hebrew, some history, and some Aristotelian physics. The logic was that of Peter Ramus, sixteenth-century French Protestant, who tried to understand concepts by dividing them into dichotomies. Every area of study could be subjected to the Ramist discipline, and the consequence was a great affection for method, for systematization. Logic, the tool of argument, went hand in hand with rhetoric, whose aim was elegance. The two were skills necessary for the public disputation that played a most important part in the academic program.

The ethics taught at Cambridge in Cotton's day was largely Aristotelian, with Aristotle's concept of the golden mean adopted as Christian good, and excess or deficiency identified as evil. With some inconsistency, the theological system that accompanied this ethics was Calvinistic. The *Institutes* of Calvin had replaced the works of the Scholastics, and nearly all English theologians were Calvinists from the 1560s until at least about 1620. Since the postbaccalaureate program was almost entirely for those intending to serve the church, theology loomed very large indeed.[3] Cotton's writings show an extensive familiarity with Calvin and his followers Junius, Beza, Piscator, Zanchius, and Martyr; with Cotton's arch-opponent the Roman Catholic Bellarmine; with the church fathers, especially Augustine; with English theologians such as Perkins, Ames, Whitaker, Jewel, Cartwright, and Whitgift; and with the Scholastics, including Thomas Aquinas. But Calvin was his special favorite. It was his grandson Cotton Mather who reports that he loved to "sweeten his mouth with a piece of Calvin" before going to sleep."[4]

Latin was the necessary tool for all scholars, but Greek and Hebrew were even more important, as the languages of Scripture. Cotton's knowledge of Hebrew was examined when he was a candidate for a fellowship of Emmanuel College, Cambridge. Norton, Cotton's early biographer, tells us that his examiner chose Isaiah 3, "which hath more hard words in it than any place in the Bible within so short a compass." Cotton did well indeed; "such was his dexterity as made those difficult words facile and rendered him a prompt respondent."[5]

After his years at Cambridge, Cotton assumed responsibility for St. Botolph's Church in Boston, Lincolnshire, despite the objection of the bishop of the diocese. St. Botolph's Church is even today worth a visit; the fourteenth-century church has been described as "the most magnificent parochial edifice in the kingdom."[6] As Cotton took on this important new post, he was described in 1614 as "but a young man not past seven or eight years M.A. but by reports a man of great gravity and sanctity of life, a man of rare parts for his learning, eloquent and well spoken."[7] The Boston Corporation Records refer to him as "a man of very good deserts" and commend "his pains in preaching" as "very great."[8] Cotton settled in Boston and married. There he trained many students who had studied at Cambridge, as well as exiled ministers from the Continent. Cotton Mather explains that "ministers driven into England by the storms of persecution then raging in Germany" came to his house; "some were sent unto him out of Germany, some out of Holland, but most out of Cambridge."[9] His preaching was so celebrated that he had to preach weekdays as well as Sundays. Something of the religious orientation of the parish is suggested by the fact that presumed members shattered the church's stained glass and destroyed the ornaments. Somehow Cotton escaped discipline. But in 1632 Cotton was at last summoned to the High Court. With "nothing but scorns and imprisonments . . . expected,"[10] he decided that he must move to the Massachusetts Bay Colony.

A devout, grace-oriented man of God, John Cotton at first had no interest in moving to America, though he preached a notable sermon to the founders of the Massachusetts Bay Colony as they departed in 1630. The Puritans of Massachusetts Bay established there a new system of church government that so distressed Cotton that he wrote to one of the ministers demanding an explanation. But just three years later, when he decided to join the colony, Cotton fully adopted the new principles of church government, as we shall see.

Because of his eminence and because some members of St. Botolph's Church had preceded him there, Cotton was made a minister in the principal town of Massachusetts, where John Winthrop, who served again and again as governor of the colony, was a member. In Boston, Cotton's preaching was so successful that he converted many and brought them into church membership. Before long, however, he found himself on the losing side of a controversy that shook the colony, when a member of his church, Anne Hutchinson, created a following and criticized many of the colony's ministers. Nevertheless, Cotton survived and indeed flourished. He was called on both to define the new system of church government and to explain it—as well as other matters—to those who had remained in the mother country. He saw the events of the world, especially the civil war in England and the resulting downfall of the king and the bishops, as signs that God was acting powerfully and significantly in history, and he provided an analysis of these events in his sermons. Till the end of his life, he preached and wrote. When he died, the records of his church described him as "the greatest star in the churches of Christ that we could hear of in the Christian world for opening and unfolding the counsels of Christ to the churches."[11]

It is time now to turn to Cotton's writings, which will be examined not chronologically but thematically.

Chapter Two
Pleader for Purity:
The Puritan Writings

John Cotton was a Puritan. This word has so many possible meanings that some effort at definition is obligatory. New England Puritanism developed when English Puritanism was permitted to be itself, cut off largely from forces unsympathetic to it. This New England Puritanism was in part what John Cotton made it, and Cotton was nearly fifty when he left England for America. For an understanding of Cotton's Puritanism, a knowledge of that of old England is vital.

English Puritanism was an effort to continue and complete the reformation of the Church of England, a project begun under Henry VIII. The uncertain path that the Church took after it separated from Roman Catholicism in 1534 became straighter when Elizabeth I ascended the throne in 1558. The path was thenceforth a middle way between the Protestantism of Calvin and traditional Catholicism. Its theology was Reformed, influenced strongly by the experiences of the church leaders who were exiled to the Continent during the reign of the Catholic Mary, though the Church retained many of the traditional practices and the episcopal hierarchy. Those who wished to "purify" the Church so that it resembled what they called the "best Reformed churches" of the Continent were labeled Puritans.

Initially, the Puritans wanted to eliminate such customs as observing saints' days, making the sign of the cross in baptism, kneeling to receive Communion, and ministers' wearing the surplice. When Elizabeth I made clear that there would be no further changes but enforced conformity to the middle way through the power of the bishops, some Puritans decided that the whole episcopal establishment should give way and that the church government, too, should be purified. They favored Presbyterianism. Most of the Puritans would have been satisfied with lesser changes; no definite Puritan program, however, was decided upon. Although Puritan hopes for better days ran high at the accession of King James in 1603, soon he made clear that he favored only minor changes. One consequence was the withdrawal of a few Puritans from the Church of England to establish separate congregations, but the majority of the Puritans did not leave the church.[1]

Both Puritans and non-Puritans within the Church of England were Calvinist until sometime after 1615. They taught that because of the sinful nature of humankind, one could be saved only if called by God to salvation. (After 1615, at least some leading Anglicans became Arminians: they believed that humankind was free to accept or reject God's grace.) The Puritans were profoundly influenced by the Continental Reformed theologian Theodore Beza, John Calvin's successor. Beza's interests were psychological; he was especially interested in the question, How does one know that he is saved? He identified the performance of good works as the preeminent sign of salvation. Instead of celebrating Christ's redeeming sacrifice, the Puritans focused their attention on the process of salvation and discovered, or thought they discovered, a pattern that could be identified.[2]

By John Cotton's time, Puritanism had four characteristics or agendas. First, Puritans sought the moral transformation of both individuals and communities. They found the world about them in England lacking order and structure. Second, Puritans urged the practice of piety, a piety characterized by preoccupation with inner spiritual states and self-discipline. Third, Puritans urged a return to the Christianity of the Bible. In place of the traditions of Catholic Christianity, some of which had been retained in the Church of England, they sought to return to the primitive past. No prayer book, no ceremonies, no ecclesiastical vestments for them. The Puritans objected to nonbiblical traditions because they judged humanity to have become so corrupted by the fall—by original sin—that whatever was human was inevitably ungodly.[3] Everything was suspect, therefore, except what the Bible prescribed. Fourth, the Puritans demanded a strict recognition of the Sabbath. This insistence was frequently a kind of badge by which Puritans could be identified.[4]

The Puritan agendas became Cotton's agendas while he was a student at Cambridge. There Thomas Cartwright had preached Presbyterianism as early as 1569. Cotton's undergraduate college was Trinity, where the influential Puritan John Udall had studied in the 1580s. But probably Cotton came under far stronger Puritan influences when in 1602 he became a fellow of Emmanuel College. Here the Master was Laurence Chaderton, one of the most persuasive of Puritans and a Puritan representative at the Hampton Court Conference with King James in 1604. In the chapel at Emmanuel, a non-prayer-book service was followed, and ministers did not wear the surplice. Holy Communion was celebrated with the receivers sitting around a table. Cotton's wholehearted acceptance of the Emmanuel practices is suggested by the fact that he served as dean, catechist, and lecturer.

During his Emmanuel years—in 1611—Cotton showed his support for a key aspect of the Puritan agenda by writing a "short discourse . . . touchinge the time when the Lordes day beginneth whether at the Eveninge or in the morninge."[5] Here Cotton argues that "in our days the Lord enlighteneth the judgment of sundry burning and shining lights especially in our English churches to see the necessity of sanctifying the Lord's day as a divine ordinance" (521). He then argues that though the Christian Sabbath has replaced the Jewish Sabbath, the Christian Sabbath should begin when the Jewish Sabbath ends, at sunset on Saturday evening. (This practice was later adopted by Puritan colonies in New England.) In addition to basing his argument on the Bible, Cotton identifies his position as that of "the practice and judgment of the primitive churches" (518).

Some Treasure

In 1612, Cotton was called to be vicar of the beautiful church of St. Botolph's in Boston, Lincolnshire, some seventy-five miles from Cambridge. Here nonconformity had been the rule for nearly thirty years. Cotton's predecessor as vicar had been found guilty of omitting the sign of the cross in baptism and of not wearing the surplice.

Despite his identification with Puritanism at Cambridge, Cotton conformed to the Church's requirements during his early years at Boston. But after a few years he decided that he could conform no longer. He therefore wrote a defense of his new position, and he apparently circulated the document among his sympathizers. He wrote at a time—about 1616–1618—when nonconformity was tolerated by those who could intelligently defend themselves. Years later, in 1660, when once again those who considered traditional ceremonies anathema needed to present their case, Cotton's statement was published, along with a work by another author, in *Some Treasure Fetched out of Rubbish: or Three short but seasonable Treatises (found in an heap of scattered Papers)*.[6]

Cotton's contribution is an answer to the question, Is it lawful for church governors to command indifferent things in the administration of God's worship? Must ministers use practices that Scripture neither requires nor forbids? Cotton's answer is no. His thoroughly Puritan view of the matter is that church governors can give orders concerning what is necessary and decent and can advise concerning what is expedient and decent; but they are not to command the indifferent and decent, because to do so is to exceed the bounds of the authority given by the apostles and to limit Christian liberty. To command the indifferent but decent is sin; to obey such commands is sin.

The Grounds and Ends of Baptisme

Although to some contemporaries the Puritans seemed to be thorough-going radicals and the Congregationalists the most radical of all, in the New World John Cotton was to argue that congregationalism was the straight and narrow middle path of truth between the corruptions of Roman Catholicism and episcopacy, on the one hand, and the intemperance, heresy, and enthusiasm of the Anabaptists and Brownists, on the other. From the days of Luther the arch-heretics had been the Anabaptists. A work that illustrates Cotton's opposition to such radicals is *The Grounds and Ends of the Baptisme of the Children of the Faithfull*, published in 1647. Cotton's prefatory letter tells us, however, that the work was written several years earlier.

A son of a member of Cotton's old church, St. Botolph's, withheld his child from baptism after reading works against infant baptism. One of these the man brought to Cotton with a request that he answer it. Because he was otherwise occupied, he handed it on to Benjamin Woodbridge, then a young scholar living with Cotton, and asked him to prepare an answer. What Woodbridge prepared was unsatisfactory, for it was too "full of scholarship and terms of art." Cotton thereupon tried his hand at a less formal approach, and years later, in America, he decided that his answer was worth publication, despite its style.

The Baptists were subject to attack from such Puritans as Cotton because they were Separatists; their practice of rebaptism indicated that they did not consider the Church of England an adequate source of things necessary for salvation. Separatists were considered seditious and schismatic; and, since their dissatisfaction with the church caused them to be identified, in the minds of some, with the Puritans, it was important for the Puritans to dissociate themselves from the Baptists. In addition, the Baptists, who tended to be drawn from the lower class, had democratic predispositions.

The dialogue form had long been a popular means of propagandizing the Puritan point of view. It had been used by Anthony Gilby, John Udall, and Arthur Dent, all influential writers. But the sense of personality and the dramatic confrontation that enliven the dialogues of these writers are quite missing in Cotton's conversation between Silvanus (Cotton) and Sylvestre (a man attracted to Baptist tenets).

It is highly significant that Cotton looks at baptism in the light of covenant theology, since it was to become associated with congregationalism and was the theology of most Massachusetts Puritan preachers. Covenant theology teaches that the children of those who had been called to God and had been admitted to the church by covenant were also within the covenant. Baptism is, for Cotton, the New Testament seal of a preexisting covenant relationship; by it, children come to be recognized as within the fellowship of the church covenant, just as circumcision was the Old Testament initiatory rite. Those within the covenant who deny baptism to their children break, therefore, the covenant between God and humankind; they keep from their children the benefits of "federal grace," which purifies the flesh and helps prevent one from lapsing back into natural depravity.[7]

Cotton teaches that children of the covenant are either the elect of God, who will absolutely be given grace, or the nonelect, to whom "He offereth to work the same in His own time, if neither their parents nor themselves reject or neglect the means which God offereth them" (20). In permitting this book to be published in the 1640s, Cotton seems to have neglected to note that it includes his outdated defense of the Anglican ministry. He denies that ministers' activities are ineffective because the bishops have usurped church powers; episcopacy had been abolished in 1643, four years before the treatise was published. He adds that ministers and laypeople should try to overcome such usurpation, but they can, if need be, "avoid it by seeking the liberty of their consciences and of their churches in some sovereign countries or plantations" (182). One wonders if Cotton was foreseeing his own future.

Because the Bishop of Lincoln, John Williams, favored him, Cotton was able to flourish at St. Botolph's Church despite his determination not to conform to the requirement of the Church of England. Another Puritan, Samuel Ward at nearby Ipswich, commented, "Of all men in the world I envy Mr. Cotton, of Boston, most; for he doth nothing in any way of conformity, and yet hath his liberty, and I do everything that way, and cannot enjoy mine."[8]

Less than a year after he preached at Southampton in 1630, Cotton and his wife became gravely ill with malaria. During their illness they stayed with Theophilus Clinton, the Earl of Lincoln, for most of a year. There Cotton was able to learn more about the Massachusetts Bay Colony, since the earl was one of its strongest supporters. There, too, Cotton's wife died. As Cotton's health improved, he traveled about and learned that the liberty of nonconformity he had enjoyed in Boston was a rare commodity. Cotton remarried, but though he expected to be able to return to St. Botolph's Church, he received word that he was being summoned to appear before the High Court. Rather than appear, he first went into hiding, then took his chances and crossed the water to Massachusetts.[9]

Of Set Forms of Prayer

When John Cotton came to America in 1633, it was almost inevitable that he should associate himself with Boston, which had been named for Boston in Lincolnshire and included among its residents many from Cotton's old town and church. Now, Cotton's self-exile permitted him to worship God in what he conceived to be the pure fashion described by Holy Scripture. In the New World, Cotton did not, however, abandon his interest in the Church of England. He defended his own practice and showed, as did others in the colony, a continuing interest in purifying the Church of England. In a letter written on 3 December 1634, to a Puritan minister who had remained in England—perhaps John Davenport—Cotton offers three reasons for his leaving England: (a) Both Cotton and Thomas Hooker (who had traveled to Massachusetts on the same ship) found that after God had "shut a door against both of us from ministering to Him and His people in our wonted congregations," they had been called "by a remnant of our people and others of this country to minister to them here." (b) They sought to bear witness to their dedication to the Puritan agenda by taking advantage of the freedom provided in America, where "there is no need of further labor in that cause." (c) They had satisfied their "souls' needs" by a mere matter of "two months' travel" and now had no further need to fight against ceremonies. Cotton has nothing to say here about the desirability of practicing congregationalism, a reason he later gave in 1651 in a preface to a book by John Norton. Puritan ministers who remained in England could continue the fight against corruption in the Church of England, he suggests, through the purity of their "own outward practice," through their counsels to their people, and by "contending for the truth," even before magistrates.[10]

Cotton's first "Puritan" publication written in America was also addressed to old England. About 1637, John Ball, a Puritan minister, sent Cotton a criticism of the New England opinion that written prayers were unlawful in church services. Ball's work (subsequently published in 1640 as *A Friendly Triall of the Grounds Tending to Separation*) asserted that a prayer is godly if its manner is holy and its matter fit, and if it deals with the needs of the supplicant. Cotton replied, according to Winthrop's *Journal*, in 1638.[11] Cotton denounced the use of all written prayers—except for the Lord's Prayer and the Psalms, both scriptural. The attack, in reality a defense of the rejection of written prayers by the Bay Colony's churches, is a ninety-page treatise entitled *A Modest and Cleare Answer to Mr. Balls Discourse of set formes of Prayer* (1642). It does not seem modest to the modern reader, for Cotton argues that, once his reader has seen Cotton's arguments, for him to persist in his errors by continuing to use written prayers is a sin against his conscience. (This same position Cotton took in explaining the seeming intolerance of the Massachusetts church, in his debate with Roger Williams.) Written prayers, creations of human imagination, are sins against the Second Commandment, for "God doth not ordinarily delight to bless the heart with gracious affections when the eyes' go a-whoring after the imaginations and inventions of men" (7). As a Puritan, Cotton looks to the Scripture to provide the precedent for church usage. To argue that the prayers of the Book of Common Prayer are expedient is to presume that "there is some help or means of God's worship expedient to the edification of the church, which never came into the hearts of Christ and His apostles to commend unto the church" (2–3).[12]

Singing of Psalmes

Akin to his work on prayer is the treatise that Cotton wrote with Thomas Shepard, *Singing of Psalmes a Gospel Ordinance* (1647), probably written years earlier. (Cotton and Shepard, not always agreed, were Boston-Cambridge neighbors.) Puritans had introduced to English worship both the singing of psalms and the use of a versified version.[13] The legitimacy of singing in churches only songs recorded in the Bible is, of course, the position for which Cotton and Shepard argue, but some exceptions are permitted. On occasions of public thanksgiving, a musically talented member of a church may sing in church a psalm he has composed; those approving it may say "amen" to it. All are to join together in singing, even women and nonmembers of the church. Why sing psalms? Cotton and Shepard explain: "that so we may sing in Sion the Lord's songs of praise according to his own will, until he take us from hence and wipe away all our tears, and bid us enter into our master's joy to sing eternal Halleluiahs."[14] It might be wise, they suggest, to line out the psalm—that is, to have someone say a line or two ahead so that those without books or unable to read may join in the singing. Musical instruments are forbidden in the church, since they are not mentioned in the New Testament; but for private singing of spiritual songs, musical accompaniment is permitted. Since the original Hebrew melodies are lost, people may invent tunes and devise meters for the psalms. Surprisingly, those preparing the musical versions are cautioned to express not only the sense but also the art of the original. Cotton and Shepard's work reveals a good deal of knowledge of poetry but less of music. Cotton's hand is especially prominent in the discussion of the musical practices of the church during its first three centuries.

Preface to *The Whole Booke of Psalmes*

Closely related to *Singing of Psalmes* is the preface to the *Bay Psalm Book*, or, as it is more properly called, *The Whole Booke of Psalmes Faithfully Translated into English Metre* (1640). Zoltan Haraszti has demonstrated Cotton's authorship of this preface, or at least a draft of it still extant, which Haraszti published in 1956 in *The Enigma of the Bay Psalm Book* (107–15). Cotton's preface appears to have been revised, perhaps by another hand, before publication. It deals with many of the questions discussed in *Singing of Psalmes.* Cotton makes plain that he favors congregational singing as opposed to singing by a choir: "if there were any other order of singing Choristers besides the body of the people to succeed those [the musicians of the Temple], the lord would doubtless have direction in the gospel for their qualification, election, maintenance, etc., as his faithfulness hath done for all other church officers in the New Testament."[15]

The translation of the psalms to be sung should, according to Cotton, be "into such verses as all our English songs run in (according to the poetry of our country)." The tunes themselves may be in the English fashion since "God hath hid from us the Hebrew temple tunes lest we should think ourselves bound to imitate them" (114). Haraszti assigns to Cotton the authorship of the translation of Psalm 23, but his case is not a very convincing one.

One of the ironies of history is that Puritanism was at its purest when it was most frustrated. In England the decay of Puritanism as a great moral and social force began with its triumph in the 1640s. In America, Puritan organicism (the concept that church, state, and society are one), though more attractive than it has appeared to some historians, was soon a highly conservative, intolerant force. It embalmed the cultural life of New England pretty effectively until the days of its rebirth—the era of Hawthorne and Emerson, both products as well as critics of Puritanism.

Chapter Three
The Means of Grace: The English Sermons

From its beginnings in the Elizabethan era, Puritanism had emphasized the importance of preaching. If the Catholic tradition puts its emphasis on the sacraments and makes the altar the focal point in the church, the Protestant tradition puts its emphasis on the sermon and makes the pulpit the focal point. Puritanism protested against the incomplete reformation of the Church of England, and, from the beginning, much of the protest was directed against the inadequacy of the preaching found in the churches. In 1559, Queen Elizabeth I admitted that very few ministers were preachers; she commanded the rest to read each Sunday one of the twelve homilies that had first been published in 1547. Though later supplemented by another collection of twenty, this was poor fare indeed. The homilies deal with such proper post-Reformation subjects as salvation by faith, the perils of idolatry, and the need to keep busy; but none of them is an exposition of Scripture. The Puritans looked to the instructions given by Saint Paul in 2 Timothy 4:2, "Preach the Word"; another favorite Puritan text, Romans 10:17, was also from Paul: "Faith cometh by hearing." Reading the Scripture or hearing a homily would not suffice; salvation required hearing sermons delivered by a godly preacher.

William Haller observes that "English Puritanism, denied opportunity to reform the established church, wreaked its energy during a half century and more upon preaching."[1] Puritan ministers were preeminently preachers, and their preaching was of many different varieties—as many varieties as there were preachers. All Puritan preachers believed it was necessary to preach both Law and Gospel, but some inevitably found themselves more insistent on God's justice and some on God's mercy. Some stressed God's love; some dwelt on what God demanded. Most, of course, stressed both. A good example of a preacher who emphasized the Law is Thomas Hooker, Cotton's fellow émigré to America. Hooker demands the most complete penitence and humility of his hearers if they would be saved. He warns them:

Hear and fear then, all you stout-hearted, stubborn and rebellious creatures, whose consciences can evidence that the day is yet to dawn, the hour yet to come, that ever you found your sins a pressure to you. They have been your pastime and delight in which you have pleased yourselves, so far from being troubled for your evils that it is your only trouble you may not commit them with content, and without control. You are troubled with admonitions, and counsels, and commands, and threatenings that cross you in your sins. You were never broken hearted here for your abominations. Know assuredly that you will burn for them one day. Your proud hearts were never abased and laid in the dust. The Lord will ruinate both you and them. Never expect a good look from God. Set your heart at rest for that.[2]

Quite different is the preaching found in many sermons of the popular Richard Sibbes, whose example Cotton followed. Sibbes was devoted to "heart" religion, to spiritual concerns, as is suggested by the fact that he frequently preached on texts from Canticles, the Song of Solomon.[3] In his *Bruised Reed and Smoking Flax*, which went through at least seven editions, Sibbes warns against preachers' demanding too much of humanity: "The ambassadors of so gentle a Savior should not be over masterly."[4]

Sibbes can preach as gently as this: "We have a mighty deliverer. He loves His children in the midst of all their deformities. Like a good father, He tenders us in our weaknesses of soul and body, and, as a father, pities His child the more for being sick. . . . He is able to help . . . in all estates; His grace is sufficient; He hath present help. What needs the child be dismayed for pain, when the Father can remove it at His pleasure?"[5] Even when his task is to warn his bearers of God's wrath, Sibbes seems hardly to raise his voice: "Little do we know what times may befall us. There is much danger abroad, and, we have cause to fear, not far from us. It may be the clouds even now hang over our heads. Oh, if we would be hid in the day of the Lord's wrath, and have no evil come nigh our dwellings, let us, above all things in the world, make sure our interest in Christ and title to the promise. We should seek to know God more, and then we would trust him more."[6]

Though the style of all Puritan preachers is usually characterized as plain, many Puritans from Henry Smith—"Silver-tongued Smith" (1557–1591) —to Robert Harris (1578–1658) were witty, though simpler and stylistically less elegant than many of their non-Puritan brethren, such as John Donne or Lancelot Andrewes. Commenting on Genesis 9:22 (Noah in his drunkenness), Smith observes: "It is said that drunken porters keep open gates. So when Noah was drunken, he set all open. As wine went in, so wit went out. As wit went out, so his clothes came off. Thus Adam, which began the world at first, was made naked with sin (Genesis 3), and Noah, which began the world again, is made naked with sin, to show that sin is no shrouder but a stripper. This is one fruit of the vine more than Noah looked for."[7] Sibbes's style lacks this ostentation; it is always directed to one purpose: "When the love of God in Christ and the benefits by Christ are laid open in preaching of the Gospel to us, God gives His Holy Spirit, the Spirit of Christ."[8] Thomas Adams (ca. 1580–1660) sets forth the proposition in more theological terms: "Such is the infallibility of God's decrees and the inseparable effects that follow His heavenly intentions that the means shall easily perform the office they were sent to do: the preaching of the Gospel shall save those whom God hath determined to save by it."[9]

As a Puritan clergyman, Cotton naturally made his reputation by his preaching. Through his sermons Cotton in fact made two reputations: one for his manner, one for his matter. The first he made in 1609 when he was a fellow of Emmanuel College, Cambridge. Though the college was already famous for its Puritanism and though Cotton identified himself with the Puritan point of view, he seems theretofore to have thought of himself primarily as a scholar. As such, probably the best way in which he could display his learning was in the pulpit. He became famous throughout the university when he delivered a funeral oration, in Latin, for the late master of Peterhouse, Robert Some. Because of his learning, Cotton developed a large following. But he did not yet consider himself to be converted, and the preacher who spoke most to him, Richard Sibbes, was a plain preacher. Through the sermons of Sibbes, Cotton found himself in 1612 called by God's grace to salvation. Now when it was his responsibility to preach again publicly, he found himself facing a dilemma. Thomas Allen tells the story as he heard it from Cotton himself, much later:

He, being according to his course to preach before the University and scholars in Cambridge, had a great conflict in himself about the composing of his sermon, viz. whether after the plain and profitable way, by raising of doctrines, with propounding the reasons and uses of the same, or after the mode of the University at that time, which was to stuff and fill their sermons with as much quotation and citing of authors as might possibly be. On the one side 'twas suggested to him that if he should not go the former way, he should not be faithful to the Lord in seeking His glory, but his own &c. And on the other side, if he should not show his learning, it would not only be a disparagement unto himself but also unto the College.[10]

Cotton chose the "plain and profitable way," much to the disappointment of some of his hearers; but, to his surprise, his preaching was responsible for the conversion of John Preston. Then a fellow of Queen's College, Preston was to

become master of Emmanuel and the most influential Puritan of his day, till
struck down prematurely in 1628. With this conversion, Cotton had evidence of the power of the plain style and adopted it permanently.

Later Cotton explained what he had learned. He abandoned the "mode of
the university" and replaced it with the "plain and profitable way" because he
recognized that "a velvet scabbard dulls the edge of the sword; it hinders the
power of it." Cotton deplored "the Word decked over with human elo-
quence." He did not want to accommodate the "itching ears" of his parishioners; he had decided that "a man is not judged by a step or two but according
to his walk and the whole drift of his course."[11]

During his years at St. Botolph's Church in Boston, Lincolnshire, and in
Massachusetts, Cotton preached thousands of sermons. John Norton tells us
that in Cotton's English days he preached on Thursdays and Fridays in the
early morning, on Saturday afternoons, and of course on Sundays. "Sometimes [he was] five or six hours in prayer and opening of the Word, so
undefatigable in the Lord's work," Norton reports.[12] In new Boston, Cotton
preached sermons on all of the Old Testament through Isaiah 30, on all of
the New Testament once, and on nearly all of it a second time. On lecture
days—weekdays when sermons were delivered—he covered many books of
both the Old and New Testaments again.

Cotton's published sermons are not necessarily his best or even representative ones, and their texts are suspect: in most cases they are reconstructions
from notes taken by hearers. Some were published without Cotton's consent,
many posthumously. Some volumes are expository sermons that treat a book
of the Bible, such as the Song of Solomon or Ecclesiastes. Some have a theme,
such as conversion and its consequences, that ties the series together even
though the texts are from various parts of Scripture. In all, there are fourteen
volumes, a total of nearly three thousand pages.

Cotton devoted twelve hours of each day to study, but in his sermons he
makes few references except to the Bible. He explained something of his view
in a letter prefixed to Arthur Hildersam's *Lectures upon the Fourth of John*
(1629):

When scholars furnish themselves with store of other writers, besides the Scriptures,
and being little conversant in the Scriptures . . . their divinity proveth but humanity,
and their ministry speaketh to the brain, but not to the conscience of the hearer. But
he that diggeth all the treasures of his knowledge and the ground of religion out of
the Scriptures, and maketh use of other authors, not for ostentation of himself, nor
for the ground of his faith, nor for the principal ornament of his ministry, but for the
better searching out of the deep wisdom of the Scriptures, such an one believeth what

he teacheth, not by an human credulity from his author, but by a divine faith from the Word, and because he believeth, he therefore speaketh, and speaking from faith in his own heart, he speaketh more powerfully unto the begetting and strengthening of faith in the hearer.

Cotton's hearers often felt that he did indeed speak from faith in his heart.

Gods Mercie Mixed with his justice

Frequently Cotton seems to have found a new theme or the beginning of a new biblical book a source of inspiration. He begins with vigor and freshness. Toward the end of nearly every volume, however, he becomes prolix and repetitious. An exception is the one volume of sermons that do not compose a series, *Gods Mercie Mixed with his justice* (1641). Matthias Swallowe, author of the prefatory epistle for Cotton's *Gods Mercie*, refers to the book as "some broken notes of his powerful soul-searching sermons taken from his mouth by the diligent hand of some well-disposed hearers and followers." Though more uniformly interesting than most of the others, these sermons, which were delivered in England, are identical in form to the others. Cotton follows the instructions provided by William Perkins in *The Arte of Prophesying*. There the preacher is instructed as follows:

1. To read the text distinctly out of the canonical Scripture.

2. To give the sense and understanding of it being read by the Scripture itself.

3. To collect a few and profitable points of doctrine out of the natural sense.

4. To apply (if he have the gift) the doctrines rightly collected to the manners of men in a simple and plain speech.[13]

Perkins explains the phrase *natural sense* by noting that "there is one only sense, and the same is the literal. An allegory is only a certain manner of uttering the same sense."[14] Another authority on the sermon explained that if the preacher finds that his text is colored by such arts as grammar and rhetoric so that its logic cannot be immediately examined, "then the words are to be stripped of those arts by some general explication, and the sense to be made plain."[15] On this issue, Cotton thought otherwise. Cotton recognized the value of figures of speech: he noted that Jesus Christ "would never have so much accustomed himself to symbols and parables, if so much was to be pared off (as husks and shells) in the interpretation . . . if parables were not effectually argumentative."[16] Cotton does not reduce metaphors to their literal meaning. If he identifies the meaning of figurative language, he (in Eugenia DeLamotte's words) "never fully substitutes those paler translations for the text."[17] To focus his listeners' attention on an image, he may quote other passages of Scripture where the same image appears, returning repeatedly to the image or metaphor. Another preacher might use a text as a springboard from which he would derive whatever significance he might determine. Not so Cotton. As Alfred Habegger notes, Cotton "opens the entire text," so that "his sermons are structures that evolve from a text."[18] Instead of reducing his text and the other Bible verses he cited to his own purposes, he (in Teresa Toulouse's words) "signified his belief in the power of the Scripture . . . to effect a complicated response."[19] The technique is not a simple one, but it can be demonstrated.

The text of the first sermon in *Gods Mercie* is Revelation 3:20: "Behold, I stand at the door and knock. If any man hear my voice and open the door, I will come in to him, and will sup with him, and he with me." This text Cotton divides into two parts: behold, which he calls a note of attention and admiration, and then the matter to be attended to. The latter he divides into three parts, each containing what he calls a double act: God's standing and his knocking; man's hearing and his opening; and God's entering and his eating. The images of God and God's actions are set before the audience. From his text Cotton draws three doctrines: "The heart of man is the door of the soul" (3). "The patience and bounty of God is great towards sinners, even admirable great in calling them home to Himself" (6); and "Such as do hear the voice and knocks of Christ and do open the door of their hearts to Him, He will vouchsafe fellowship with them, familiar and continual fellowship with them, feasting of them and be feasted by them" (20). In setting forth each doctrine, Cotton provides word pictures.

Next, each of the doctrines is explained, partly by referring to parallel ideas found elsewhere in Scripture, partly by showing in detail what the implications of the doctrine are. For example, Cotton explains that God's patience (referred to in the second doctrine) is manifested in his restraint in punishing the sinner, in his issuing warnings before he punishes, in his delaying after issuing warnings, and in his restraint even in punishing.

Next come the reasons for the doctrine: *why* the heart is called the door, *why* God is so patient. Finally come the uses, or practical implications, of the doctrines. The doctrine that the heart of a person is the door of his or her soul shows that knowledge and wisdom count for nothing. If God is so patient, how ashamed should the person be who has not repented! If God grants fellowship to those who open their hearts to him, what good reason there is to repent and accept God!

What is exceptional about Cotton is that he does not follow rigidly the pattern of text, doctrine, reasons, and uses. For him, the imagery lends itself to development, and Cotton takes full advantage of the possibilities. Instead of offering a systematic reading of the verse, Cotton identifies a wide range of possibilities and associations, drawing on other texts, such as John 10:9, "I am the door; by me if any man enter in, he shall be saved." Cotton seems to suppose that among the many possibilities he offers, each individual in his audience will find one that speaks to him or her. As Toulouse observes, "in displaying a variety of possible logical, psychological, and spiritual meanings," Cotton "is closely suggesting the richness of God's revelation, not rigidly controlling its interpretation."[20]

In the second sermon in *Gods Mercie*, "The Saints Deliverance," the technique is even more striking. The text is this metaphorical description of the "saints" from Revelation 7:14: "These are they which came out of great tribulation, and have washed their robes and made them white in the blood of the Lamb." This passage inspired Cotton to produce these words:

[P]oor men, yes, yet they were adorned with robes. Had it not been enough to say "washed their garments"? What, must poor men be set up with robes? Yet robes they have, and white robes, and they washed in the blood of the Lamb. So that it shows you that the servants of God that come well out of tribulations, they get more royal spirits than ever before, for robes become royal persons and princes. When robes in good earnest are put upon any, they put upon them princely majesty; a spirit of glory and royalty is put upon them. He carries himself no more like a base drudge of this world. He is able to over-wrestle all tribulations and afflictions of this world. (39)

Cotton stays with the metaphor of his text. Though he "translates" the metaphor, he does not abandon it. By emphasizing the figurative language, he requires his hearers to hold the imagery in their minds. Even at the end of a sermon, in the "uses," he returns to the imagery he has developed: "If you were to pull a child out of mire, one of your first works would be to put other clothes upon him. God doth so to his servants, and the mire he turns into soap and makes it clean us" (46). As Toulouse observes, "Cotton is far less interested in following out a progressive, self-evident, deductive program than he is in exploring varying ways of viewing" analogies, images, metaphors.[21]

What does Cotton accomplish by this technique? He addresses not merely the understanding but the heart, the affections, through the repeated imagery. He provides his listeners not only with words, with sounds, but with pictures to see, pictures of robes, with kinesthetic imagery as well, with the sensation of wearing robes. Cotton does not dilute his sermons by translating the metaphors of his text into simple logic. Instead he induces his listeners to enter the world of his metaphors, as in the following passage from "The Wickeds' Craft," another sermon in *Gods Mercie*. Cotton's text is Matthew 16:1–3, the relevant portion being this: "The Pharisees with the Sadducees came, and tempting desired him that he would show them a sign from heaven." From this image, Cotton draws a picture:

This is one sign of the time of our visitation, when God begins . . . to shine upon us by the light of his Gospel and the beams of his Spirit and knocks thereby at our hearts, and yet we love to sleep and will draw about us the curtains of carnal security and of our own lusts. Now it is high time to awake. O ye hypocrites, can ye tell when to arise in the morning and when to go about your business and to stir yourselves about your labors, and cannot you tell when it is time to awake out of your blind courses, wherein you have lain so many years together? (122)

Cotton's hearers find themselves in bed when it is time to be stirring. They are encouraged to get up—to recognize that they have been given the sign they have been seeking. Cotton has been creating "a bridge between the Scriptural text and his listeners' hearts."[22]

Gods Mercie is a good introduction to Cotton as a preacher because it shows us his concept of God. The title, presumably chosen by the author of the prefatory epistle, Matthias Swallowe, suggests that Cotton's God is both merciful and just; and, indeed, the sermons—like those of Sibbes—all suggest God's patience, mercy, concern, and restraint. Cotton's God is much more attractive, much less inclined to terrify a congregation than the God of most of his contemporaries is; and in this respect Sibbes's influence seems clear. It is the sermon technique, the use of imagery, that is original.

A Brief Exposition Of the Whole Book of Canticles

Much of *Gods Mercie* remains interesting; it is probably as attractive as any volume of sermons we have from Cotton. The volume is brief (135 pages) and is available in a modern facsimile edition. Very different is Cotton's *A Brief Exposition Of the Whole Book of Canticles, or Song of Solomon* (1642), which requires attention to its historical context. The exegesis was notable in its day. The subject was considered not only fascinating but crucial for an understanding of how God was acting in current affairs. After Cotton's death, a second series of his sermons on the same text, delivered in America, was published. In the later volume, prepared by Cotton, he reports that the 1642 volume was published "without my privity" (2).

The poetry of the Song of Solomon has made it a very attractive book; Christians have frequently read it as an allegory of Christ and the church. Reading the book as history did not originate with Cotton. The practice goes back to the Talmud, and the Targum (an Aramaic paraphrase of Scripture) provides a detailed allegorical interpretation. Adopted by the Christian church, the allegorical reading was not seriously questioned until the time of Erasmus. Thomas Brightman, an English clergyman, prepared a famous commentary, published in 1614, in which he contended that the book is a detailed prophetic history of the church from the reign of David till the end of the world. Cotton was influenced by Brightman but argued that the prophecy began in Solomon's reign. Like Brightman, Cotton reads verses as providing a very precise prophecy of events that were to come.[23] His commentary prefigures his later interest in millennialism such as he demonstrates in his American sermons on texts from the Book of Revelation. Dwight Bozeman identifies the 1642 work as "an unmistakably proto-millennial statement," with "no counterpart" in the writings of other clergymen who came to America (I cite the London edition of 1642).[24]

On the first page of his explanation of the Song of Songs, Cotton comments on the first verse, "The song of songs, which is Solomon's," that "Solomon was, first, a type of Christ," then explains why: "he is set forth as the desire, praise, and blessedness of all his people" (3, 20). Here Cotton is applying a method of biblical interpretation known as typology. Typology is based upon several important passages in the New Testament, notably the following: "For as Jonas was three days and three nights in the whale's belly, so shall the Son of man be three days and three nights in the heart of the earth" (Matthew 12:40); "I would not that ye should be ignorant, how that all our fathers were under the cloud, and all passed through the sea; and were all baptized unto Moses in the cloud and in the sea; and did all eat the same spiritual meat; and did all drink the same spiritual drink, for they drank of that spiritual Rock . . . and that Rock was Christ. . . . [N]ow all these things happened unto them for ensamples" (1 Corinthians 10:1–4, 11). The Greek word translated *ensamples* is *typoi*. The same word appears also in Romans 5:14: "Nevertheless, death reigned from Adam to Moses . . . who is the figure [*typos*] of him that was to come." Later, several of the early Greek and Latin church fathers developed the method, which was also used in the Reformation by Martin Luther and John Calvin.[25] Among Puritans, William Ames in his *Medulla Sacrae Theologiae* (1612), later translated as *The Marrow of Sacred Theology*, includes a chapter entitled "The Administration of the

Covenant of Grace before the Coming of Christ," which provides an interpretation of Old Testament ceremonies as prefiguring and adumbrating the sanctification available through grace. Ames argued that "Christ and redemption were foreshadowed by the high priest, the altars, and sacrifices for sins."[26] It was left for other Puritans, notably John Cotton, to extend their reading of the Old Testament by interpreting it as foreshadowing or prophesying not only the events of the New Testament but also post–New Testament Christian history. This is what Cotton attempts in his *Brief Exposition*. Cotton emphasizes the continuity of the Old Testament past, the events of the New Testament, and the events of ecclesiastical history up to his own time—and beyond. He refers to the "church" as a phenomenon beginning in Old Testament times and continuing.[27]

Cotton declares that he is aware that the Song of Solomon is regarded by some as sensuous, but he reproves such an attitude. He rejects as well the ancient synagogue law prohibiting men under thirty from reading the book, for Cotton believes that it can only fire young men with heavenly love; to him it is "a divine abridgment of the acts and monuments of the church" (9). The history that the book is said to describe seems somewhat less clear than Cotton found it. He finds, for example, prophecy in the ninth verse of the first chapter: "I have compared thee, O my love, to a company of horses in Pharaoh's chariots." Here we have, says Cotton, a description of the condition of the church of Judah after Rehoboam fell away so that God sent Shishak of Egypt to subdue Judah. To support this view, Cotton reminds his audience that Shishak caused kings to draw his chariots like horses.

Presumably, one of the reasons that Cotton was unhappy to see his own book in print after he had left England for America was that he was embarrassed by his interpretation of the fifth verse of the first chapter: "I am black but comely." This verse is useful, declares Cotton, because it teaches "the children of the Church not to separate from the Church for corruption's sake . . . but to see her comeliness also" (30–31). He further comments, "It was a sin in them to be angry with the Church as some of the separatists are, and do depart from us. . . . What and if some cast off England? Shall we reject it because some of the sons of her mother do?" (31–32). Throughout the work, Cotton is a vigorous opponent of separatism.

Cotton shows his Congregationalist tendencies by his definition of the church as "an assembly of many good Christians or saints . . . set in order . . . amongst whom Christ walketh, they enjoying fellowship with Him in His public ordinances, and He with them" (180). "Such churches," Cotton explains, "and congregations are queens whom the ministers and congregations do with mutual free consent choose either the other; as when the people do give up themselves first to the Lord and then to the ministers by the will of God. Of this sort are sundry congregations in England, and very many in the Reformed sovereign churches. Other congregations which have ministers thrust upon them without their liking and consent, and whom ministers have to them by some clandestine conveyances, are more like to concubines" (185).

While in England, Cotton thus clearly adumbrated his later views, though of course he was less strict in his requirements for a true church. Unlike most Puritans, who thought of the Christian church in England in terms of the national Church of England, Cotton considered the church as a particular church. He lists the requisites for a church: free acceptance and maintenance of the minister by the people, powerful preaching, discipline (specifically the power of excommunication), and the discovery of saints through preaching.

The collection of sermons in *Brief Exposition* is marked by many observations of interest to the student of Cotton, but since in a later volume on the same book of Scripture Cotton provided a fuller and more mature treatment of the subject and a better text, we leave this book—which amounts to a collection of notes—after this slight consideration.

The way of Life

The longest of Cotton's sermon volumes is *The way of Life, Or God's Way and Course, in bringing the Soule into; keeping it in, and carrying it on, in the wayes of life and peace* (1641). This volume, too, according to the prefatory epistle, was published without Cotton's knowledge. The sermons were delivered in England: Cotton complains of those who "come to offer their children in baptism; they never consider what they have in hand; come only to take the rites of the Church and what the laws of the kingdom require; put God off with mere compliments" (389). Such a situation Cotton never permitted in America.

This volume resembles many other Puritan treatises on conversion, for example, those of Cotton's American colleagues Thomas Hooker and Thomas Shepard. (But as we shall see, in America Cotton's position was distinctively different from both Hooker's and Shepard's.) Cotton's sermon collection is ostensibly an objective description of the salvation process, as the title suggests. In reality *The way of Life* is intended to provide the means of salvation; for, as the fourteenth chapter of the Westminster Confession puts it, "the grace of faith, whereby the elect are enabled to believe to the saving of their souls, is the work of the Spirit of Christ in their hearts and is ordinarily wrought by the ministry of the Word." Or, as Cotton declares in this volume,

God gives grace to those who seek it, especially to those who seek it in sermons: "If God give thee but an heart to feel thine own want . . . He will give
you a Spirit of grace"(12).

According to Cotton, one knows that God has given him grace when he
recognizes his own sinfulness and loathes himself. One recognizes, too, the
deadly forces that surround him—the flesh, his own doubts, his coldness of
heart, his pride and wrath—and from these he seeks relief from God through
prayer. He prays for a soft and believing heart, a humble spirit, and sanctifying grace. This eagerness to pray and the ability to do so are, for Cotton,
God's gifts of grace.

As Cotton proceeds, the method becomes clearer. How does one know if
he is saved? By seeing whether he can do what the preacher says can be done
only with God's grace. This approach neatly reconciles a willingness to acknowledge the salvation process as God's work with the practical fact that
the minister must urge his hearers to act. Cotton's description of the second
effect of God's saving grace also demonstrates this reconciliation. Through
grace, says Cotton, God gives a person power to see that he has crucified
Christ and to recognize that through the Crucifixion there is redemption.

The subsequent effects of saving grace that Cotton describes are sufficiently unnatural to relieve Cotton of the charge of preaching "bootstraps
theology" pure and simple. He who receives God's grace, says Cotton, sor-
rows for sin so much that he can be said to go into a mourning greater than
that appropriate for the loss of an only child: "The spirit of grace helping us to
mourn, it will make our grief to grow, to be more at the last than at the
first. . . . It lasts while life lasts" (54).

Perhaps because he recognized that he was making it sound very difficult
to be saved, Cotton describes the times as a period when God is giving his
grace with peculiar abundance—and to the worst of people. Thus Cotton
tried to encourage all of his hearers, especially those far from God, to seek humiliation. The reward for true humiliation is assurance of salvation: "Dost
thou find thy will and inclination to [sin] die and decay in thee so as that thou
hast no desire or delight in sin? The liveliest spirit thou hast to this or that sin
is now evaporated and wasted, and thy heart is furnished with graces opposite to those sins? . . . If it be thus with thee, then surely God hath pierced thy
heart, and thou art in an estate of salvation" (130).

Though much of Cotton's preaching is evangelical and addressed therefore to the sinner whom he would save by encouraging penitence, Cotton
speaks also to those who have previously felt themselves called. He uses analogies to suggest personal application: if God does not speak to a man's sins in
a sermon, says Cotton, he is like a child not remembered in his father's will.

By such means, Cotton sought to bring home to his audience that they were in the presence of the means of grace whenever they were hearing a sermon.

Cotton brightens up his discourse by the use of visual images. He compares the means of grace, the sermon, to a sword: "The sword of God, take it as it lies in the Word, and it is like a sword in the scabbard, and the exposition is but the brandishing of it; but when application is made, that thou art the man that has done this, not to endure this is an argument of a carnal heart, though sometimes even God's own people do not love to be particularized" (171–72). This last phrase suggests the gentleness and tender-mindedness found throughout most of these sermons. But in the sermons on Acts 2:37, Cotton resolves to be firm. He preaches on contrition, which is necessary since "the very first work of living and saving grace gives a deadly stroke to the life of sinful nature" (125). Perhaps this is his strongest passage:

A direction and advertisement to such as yet find their hearts whole and unbroken: take heed how you content yourselves in such a condition. Consider what our Savior said to Saul, "It is hard to kick against the pricks"; to dash the naked soul against the curse and wrath of God is a hard business. . . . [B]ut many a man that goes on in sin saith he feels no such hard work in sin. But thou wilt feel at the last that it hath been but dashing against pricks, and if not in this world, then with more horror in another. You little know what anguish of soul for sin means. Can you provoke God to anger and not yourselves to confusion? (132–33)

At his toughest, Cotton remains gentle; he can scarcely be said to have put the wrath of God before his hearers.

Cotton's mildness is even more striking when one turns to Thomas Hooker's sermons on the same text. Hooker suggests that God is sometimes merciful to sinners and might be merciful to some of the sinners present. Then he exclaims: "Oh, is it not pity to cast such dainties before dogs, and pearls before swine? Did I say it was possible? True, I said so, indeed, but it's pity thou wert in the hearing of it. It's pity to speak such precious encouragements to such poisonous and malignant spirits that will pervert all to their own ruin. The word is past and cannot be recalled, but take these preservatives, or corrosives, rather, to eat out that impudent corruption."[28]

At times Cotton reveals, unwittingly, the difficulty of reconciling the theory that conversion is God's work with the need to be exhortatory in preaching. He argues, against the semi-Pelagian Roman Catholic position, that experience proves that the followers of Calvin are right in teaching that God's grace is irresistible: "The people of God can tell [that] when God first looked into their hearts they were most drowsy at such a sermon, and their hearts

more wandering that day than ordinary, and so unfit for mercy in themselves"
(182). But Cotton would not have those who have not yet been called sit and
drowse through his sermons. He asks his hearers to reflect: "Have I lived here
in a congregation where I have been followed with means of grace almost
these eighty years, and know not to this day in what estate my poor soul
stands before God? Now take it to heart, and see how you will answer this to
God. Never rest and sleep in such a condition lest in the end you be past
remedy" (184).

Another seeming inconsistency in Cotton's preaching is that he speaks of
the need of the preacher to be specific, to point to sins and name them; yet he
is thoroughly vague. For example, in part of this collection of sermons, in the
226-page "The Life of Faith," Cotton frequently refers to "a Christian holy
life." The character of this life is never specifically described; the phrase seems
to mean going to church diligently, attending to the sacraments and the sermon, reading the Bible, and forsaking one's (unspecified) lusts. Students of
economic history, such as Tawney, have frequently remarked that Puritanism
encouraged capitalism. One of the men who by Cotton's own testimony
taught him much, Paul Baynes, had this to say about the relationship of pros-
perity and goodness: "Observe that the next [nearest] way for a man to thrive
in his outward state is first to grow rich in his spiritual. . . . God doth undertake to keep damage from his, while they are occupied in his service."[29] One
can see that Cotton's teachings, too, might encourage a spirit of individual
enterprise. According to Cotton, a Christian may be

busy in his calling from sun rising to sun setting, and may by God's providence fill
both his hand and head with business yet a living Christian when he lives a most busy
life . . . he lives not a worldly life. (270)

That God may be glorified in Jesus Christ, this is the sum of his eating and drinking
and buying and selling &c.; this is the upshot of all; this is all for Christ. (271–72)

The more God blesseth a man with a fair estate, the more doth faith quicken him to
fear and serve God and enlarges him thereunto. (457)

Diligence in one's vocation is so supremely important for Cotton that he
conceives of it as the outward parallel to the inward life of faith, the life of
prayer and thankfulness, and the hearing of sermons: "As soon as ever a
man begins to look towards God and the ways of His grace, he will not rest
till he find out some warrantable calling and employment. . . . A Christian

would no sooner have his sin pardoned than his estate to be settled in some good calling" (437).

Though Cotton connects diligence in one's vocation with Christian responsibility, and though he is painfully vague concerning most of humanity's other responsibilities, he makes clear that at the time he prepared these sermons he was no Antinomian—he did not believe that one was free to reject grace. He always assumes an intimate connection between faith and good works, between redemption and sanctification—the kind of relationship that Anne Hutchinson later called a Covenant of Works. Part of Cotton's "legal" preaching is his comment on Galatians 2:20, "I am crucified with Christ; nevertheless I live; yet not I, but Christ liveth in me; and the life which I now live in the flesh I live by the faith of the Son of God, who loved me and gave himself for me":

There is no man who seeks righteousness by Christ but he destroys the body of sin; no man partakes in justification by Christ but he is crucified with Christ, and justified by faith in Christ Jesus; there is no man weaned from sin more than such men, no man more weaned from the things of this world, nor so much, as he that is justified by faith in Christ Jesus. No man hath fellowship with Christ in His death pardoning his sin but he hath fellowship with Him also purging him from sin. (262–63)

A Commentary on First John

The sermons in *The way of Life* are tied together by their theme; many are in fact on the same text. Much less unified is the volume of sermons entitled *A Practical Commentary or an Exposition with Observations, Reasons, and Uses upon The First Epistle Generall of John.* Though not published until 1656, this thick volume contains sermons evidently delivered in England, as a passage shows: "Tell a child of some thing—let but his father say, he will buy him such a thing at London, or he hath it laid up for him, he rests well pleased" (85). And Cotton speaks of "we in England" (156). Also, the prefatory letter reports that an Essex minister had heard most of the sermons. It is possible to date these sermons more precisely, for Cotton refers to the death of John Preston, which occurred in 1629. Thus, they are from 1629 to 1632.[30]

Cotton appears to have had in mind the presence of divinity students in his congregation, some of whom had come to him after studying with Preston, who "would advise his near fledged pupils to go to live with Mr. Cotton, that they might be fitted for public service."[31] Perhaps for this reason there are many passages on rhetoric in these sermons. But the wide variety of the subject matter of these sermons can only be suggested: the composition of the

Bible, Roman Catholic traditions, the teachings of the church fathers, morality, history, and, most extensively, fellowship with God. Unlike many of Cotton's other sermons, these display somewhat ostentatiously their author's
extensive reading. He repeats the Schoolmen's reasons that Christ did not become an angel to save the fallen angels. He considers what the Father and the
Son did in the period before the world was created, said to be five thousand
years before the time when Cotton was preaching. He criticizes the church fathers because they did not know Hebrew. And he discusses the religious significance of lots:

[A]ll lots are religious, whether they be about Holy things, as choosing apostles, or
civil, as casting lots about division of lands, or any other thing, to determine controversy or the like, as they cast lots for Christ's garments, for it is not the object that
makes a thing lawful or unlawful, as whether we swear in religious or civil matters, or
lusory [gaming], because whatsoever we swear about, we call God to be a witness, so
in all kinds of lottery, whatsoever it be about, we appeal to God, who is disposer of
all things (Proverbs 16.33), for man being but *causa per accidens* of the event of the
lot, there must be some cause *per se*, and that is God, for whatsoever it be about,
though matters of pastime or lusory, it is a religious ordinance because it appeals to
divine providence, and therefore is to be avoided. (127)

The subject of lots interested the Puritans; Thomas Gataker, a contemporary
of Cotton, wrote *Of the Nature and Use of Lots* (1619), an entire treatise on
the subject.

Once again, Cotton in this collection reveals his early views on the church
and congregationalism. He defends both the reading of prayers and the
Church of England, but he admits that the Church has weaknesses. They are
failures not in fundamental doctrine but only in "the skirts and some circumstances" (157). The chief problem is the relationship of minister and people.
Cotton protests that even this difficulty is not universal: "many of us are
elected by the people's approbation, or by such as are set up by the king and
state, and if God bless our ministry to convert thousands to God by that
means, it is an evident sign God approves our calling, for if it were anti-
Christian they would not convert souls to God" (157). Cotton speaks here
against the Separatists again. In this volume, Cotton once again gives great
emphasis to the role of good works. (He taught otherwise when he came to
America.) He teaches emphatically that good works do not justify a person,
yet by them "we know that we are justified," and he says, "If a man walks in a
constant course of obedience to God's commandments, he may thereby
know that he is in Christ, and this must needs be an encouragement to works"

(72). Cotton comes as close in this instance as anywhere to preaching a doctrine of salvation by works.

More orthodox is his gloss on 1 John 2:2, "And He is the propitiation for our sins, and not for ours only, but also for the sins of the whole world." Cotton comments: "Jesus Christ is the propitiation for the sins not only of believing Jews but likewise of believing Christians all the world over." Here Cotton teaches the High Calvinist doctrine of the limited atonement.

From time to time in this volume of sermons appear passages that are so laced with biblical citations as to make the work almost unreadable. Thus Cotton comments that the Incarnation was "the manifestation of Him [Christ] to the inward man; for though they knew Him to be God (Psalm 110:1), mark our Savior's urging that place (Matthew 22:44, 45) and man (Genesis 3:15) to be of His Church, the King (Psalm 2:8, 9), the Priest (Psalm 110:4, Daniel 9:17), the Prophet (Deuteronomy 18:18, Job 4:25)" (13). This practice of citing is rather too common, and it keeps the work from having any literary value.

Christ The Fountaine of Life

Closely related to this commentary are the sixteen sermons that make up *Christ The Fountaine of Life; or, Sundry Choyce Sermons on part of the fift Chapter of the first Epistle of St. John.* The reason that Cotton could lavish so much attention on just six verses when he had devoted the makings of a book of sermons to the entire five chapters of 1 John appears to be that the sermons of *Christ The Fountaine* were lecture-day addresses, and on these days he chose to focus on a theme with which his text dealt, instead of offering, as he did on Sundays, a full commentary on his text.

Cotton's central theme in these sermons is that Saint John's identification of Christ with life means that without Christ, one's sins merit death, that justification is the price of eternal life. The sanctified life, the effect of justification, is also to be understood as the life that is identified with Christ. The specifically Puritan character of Cotton's work is manifested by the fact that ten of the sermons are devoted to the problem that was to become central in the Antinomian Controversy in Massachusetts: How can one tell if he possesses Christ and thereby possesses life? The need for proof was central in the strict predestination atmosphere; fatalism would be the logical outcome of predestinarian teaching except for what Max Weber calls "the idea of proof": "Because of it the psychological result was precisely the opposite."[32] The strenuous efforts that Weber implies, by which one demonstrates that he is among the elect, are fully prescribed by Cotton, who explains that one who possesses Christ prizes him above all else and abases himself; desires to know Christ and his power to be gracious; is affected by Christ in the heart, the will, and the affections; does Christ's will; and respects every commandment of God as a means of honoring and worshiping Christ.

Cotton once again emphasizes the importance of the heart. He argues that a person "worships Christ not only by an act of his mind, but a man hath Christ likewise when he hath him in the deep affection of his heart, as his chiefest good. The former was an act of the judgment and understanding; this belongs to the heart, will, and affections" (9). Then one notes a subtle shift in Cotton's point of view. In the second sermon, he describes not so much how one knows whether he possesses Christ but how to possess him. Although several ways are suggested, Cotton of course leaves in each case some initiative to God. If emphasis on proof, however, encourages human efforts, it is fair to say that Cotton teaches in this sermon something very close to voluntarism. He argues, for example, that when God

sees men are willing to forgo their most darling, delightful sins, willing to break off all impediments that stand between God and them, the soul of God is grieved in such a case, and it pities Him now that such a soul should be without Him; and then it will not be long ere God stirs up means of deliverance, and He Himself will reveal Himself unto them. . . . God is then abundantly ready to pardon, when men forsake their own ways and thoughts, and throw away the sins that hang about them. (20)

. . . [W]hen we come to God, and desire Him not only to take them [our sins] from us but begin to consider our own ways and iniquities and to put them from us, out of our hearts and hands . . . then the Lord presently gives us the Lord Jesus Christ, and life and healing in Him. (21)

Although much has sometimes been made of the covenant concept as a crucial part of the salvation process in Puritan preaching, Cotton describes it as merely one of the several ways by which people may come to possess Christ, and it is as demanding a way as any. In fact, Cotton almost makes the covenant a Covenant of Works rather than of faith, for the terms of the covenant include promising to do God's will and sacrificing one's self—one's soul and one's body. The covenant Cotton refers to here differs from what Cotton elsewhere calls the Covenant of Works only in that one who breaks the covenant finds that God is willing to reseal it after confession and repentance.

Another indication of how much Cotton's views changed later in life may be mentioned here. In the third sermon of *Christ The Fountaine* Cotton teaches that Christ will enter one's heart if one prepares the way for him by humility, by loving Christ, by being willing to do whatever Christ would have one do, by believing that there is hope for one, and by casting out all lusts. In the eighth sermon Cotton teaches that to go willingly to Christian duties argues that one is of the elect. By the time Cotton delivered the sermons in the later *A Treatise of the Covenant of Grace* (1659) he was determined to emphasize not a person's ability but the necessity of God's grace in the salvation process. Thus, he argues in these later sermons that the whole process of salvation, even the preparatory steps, is God's work and that "any saving preparation in the heart" is a sign of election (39–40).

That the difference between Cotton's English teachings and his American ones is a matter of emphasis is suggested by the precise formulation of a modern student of reformed theology, Heinrich Heppe, who offers this clear, though sophisticated, explanation:

[T]he Holy Spirit so works upon man as to esteem him a personal creature and so does not regard him as a clod or a stone, but acts so that enlightened by the Word and impelled by grace man receives in conversion the will to convert to God and so his conversion takes the form of spontaneity. Yet since in conversion every sort of cooperation of man's will with the Holy Spirit is completely excluded, the activity therein exercised by the Holy Spirit is no merely natural, merely moral or mediate activity (no mere *suasio per verbum* [verbal persuasion]), but at the same time and preeminently an immediate, supernatural one, in which the Holy Spirit avails itself of the Word as its means, yet, in a way completely independent of the natural activity of the Word, works essentially and irresistibly upon the thought, will, and life of man.[33]

Cotton puts the matter somewhat similarly in *Christ The Fountaine* when he defends exhortation of the unconverted: "for though in nature we are neither willing nor able to look after Christ, but look at Him as a vain refuse commodity . . . God many times conveys such a Spirit of grace into us as gives us power to receive Christ" (173). He argues that "no saving gift of God can be wrought in the heart without faith, and . . . faith comes . . . by hearing" (181).

The difference between John Cotton's English sermons and those of other preachers of his tradition is that Cotton is more cautious. He does not promise his hearers that if they prepare for the coming of Christ, Christ will come and save them, as does Thomas Hooker:

You see the means that God appointed for the conveyance of grace and mercy to you, nay, that Christ Himself may take possession of you, and it is the way and means that never will deceive you. Would you have Christ to dwell in you? Then be humbled and be not wanting to yourselves, and then Christ will never be wanting to you. Labor to get this humiliation, and Christ will come immediately into your souls. Have a heart but rightly disposed, and without all question Christ will come to comfort and refresh thee upon all occasions.[34]

We have seen how demanding a preacher Hooker was; perhaps he thought that by demanding much he could promise much. Cotton asked less and promised less: "[T]his is the preparation we must make for Christ to come unto us. You have sometimes heard this fully spoken to, that is, when the high mountains of our great spirits and lofty looks are brought so low that we are content to be nothing in our own eyes, that we have all we have in Christ, and are able to bring nothing to Him, and are willing that He should do with us what is good in His own eyes; then these high mountains being brought low, we are made fit for Christ to come in to us" (41).

John Calvin himself is less demanding than Cotton, and Calvin promises quite as much as Hooker: "when we shall be well persuaded that it is to those who are most miserable that He addresses the salvation which He acquired, provided they recognize themselves as such, and they humble themselves, and they are entirely confounded, rendering themselves blameworthy (as they are) before the judgment of God; that is how we shall have easy access to be sharers of the righteousness which is offered to us, and by which we obtain grace and favor before God."[35]

Christ The Fountaine once again demonstrates Cotton's inability to sustain his interest (or at least the interest of this reader) throughout the series. But even late in the volume one finds an occasional attractive passage, such as this one, which provides an analogy:

As if an elder brother should set a child, one of his younger brethren, to get his father a posey, of flowers, and the child out of ignorance should gather some weeds and put [them] in it, and the elder brother gathers out the weeds and sprinkles the flowers and then presents them in the child's name to the father; so doth Christ to us, while we gather up petitions here and there, and, as we think, for the best, and some truth and work of grace there is in them, yet some weeds of sinful folly, then Christ takes them out of your hands and pulls out the weeds and sprinkles them with the blood of His cross. (223–24)

In New England, Cotton attracted followers who took great satisfaction from their spiritual experiences. Whereas other ministers would have the members of their churches examine and reexamine their behavior to see evidence of salvation, Cotton emphasized the religious gratifications available to the converted.[36] A striking specimen of such a concern is this passage from *Christ the*

Fountaine: God will "pour out his Spirit in a rich and plentiful measure. . . . [W]hen comes it to pass that the servants of God understand many secrets of God's counsel . . . many a godly man by the same Spirit discerns many secret mysteries and meanings of the Holy Ghost in Scripture mire than ever he could by any reading or instruction" (62). Such teaching empowers the private person, who is unlikely to imagine that ministerial instruction is of much significance compared with the direct instruction provided by the Spirit.

Gods Promise to his Plantation

The most famous and doubtless the most interesting of Cotton's English sermons is *Gods Promise to his Plantation . . . As it was delivered in a Sermon* (1630).[37] The occasion was the departure of John Winthrop and four hundred others on the *Arbella*, bound for Massachusetts from Southampton. It was Cotton's first sermon to be published and is often placed alongside the sermon that John Winthrop preached at sea, "Christian Charity."

Cotton's carefully chosen text was 2 Samuel 7:10: "Moreover I will appoint a place for my people Israel, and I will plant them that they may dwell in a place of their own and move no more." After describing the historical situation in 2 Samuel, Cotton explains how God makes room for a people by casting out the people's enemies by war, or by arranging for them to be given a portion by courtesy, or by emptying a land of its inhabitants so that it is vacant. (The English could not have known that the plague that had so reduced the Indian population of New England had been brought about by the importation of diseases to which the Native Americans had no immunity.) Cotton argues that if God appoints a land for colonists to live in, they have a religious responsibility to live there. Cotton then describes six circumstances in which it is proper for a people to emigrate—all six presumably relevant for the colonists. They may move to gain knowledge; to conduct merchandising; "to plant a colony, that is, a company that agree together to remove out of their own country, and settle a city or commonwealth elsewhere" (8); to employ their talents better; to obtain "the liberty of the ordinances" as in the days of Queen Mary or "when some grievous sins overspread a country that threaten desolation"; or to take advantage of a special providence "if sovereign authority command and encourage such plantations by giving way to subjects to transplant themselves and set up a new commonwealth" (9). The special terms of the colonists' charter gave them, as Cotton seemed to recognize, remarkable freedom to undertake an ambitious political, social, and religious revolution in the new land. There is no indication that Cotton sees the creation of the colony as a vital aspect of the coming of the millennium, as some have argued.[38] But he did see that England's corruption was to be avoided: "Tradesmen no longer live one by another, but eat one another up" (8).

The most interesting part of the sermon is the advice that Cotton offers to the new colonists. Of course, Cotton emphasizes the importance of church "ordinances": preaching, discipline, and the sacraments. But he reminds the colonists also: "Be not unmindful of our Jerusalem at home, whether you leave us, or stay at home with us. . . . Forget not the womb that bare you and the breast that gave you suck" (14). He asks that the colonists care for their children, who in a new land might well become degenerate. But it is the possibility that the colonists might become effective missionaries that captures Cotton's imagination: "Offend not the poor natives, but as you partake in their land, so make them partakers of your precious faith. As you reap their temporals, so seed them with your spirituals. Win them to the love of Christ, for whom Christ died. They never yet refused the Gospel, and therefore more hope they will now receive it. Who knoweth whether God have reared this whole plantation for such an end?" (19–20). Cotton's hopes for the Indians were not, of course, realized. Later, when he became the great apologist for the colony, he was particularly sensitive to the failure of the Indian missionary effort. His explanation was that conversion of the Indians, in God's scheme of things, must await the conversion of the Jews.[39]

The reader of Cotton's English sermons may very well be curious to see what changes took place in his sermon technique and his approach with a different audience and a different setting. But we should remember that he was almost fifty when he left England for America; his patterns and methods were well established.

Chapter Four

Champion of the New England Way: The Congregational Writings

John Cotton's most important task in the New World was that of spokesman for the new form of church government that developed in Massachusetts Bay Colony. He was the first to make use of the word *Congregational* as descriptive of his notion of what was a proper church.[1] Although scholars differ on the historical background of American congregationalism, they do agree that the adoption of this church polity was of particular importance and had significant consequences.

Congregationalism in time was responsible for the development of a sense of spiritual separation from England quite as great as the physical separation, and this sense did much to give New England its peculiar moral strictness and its occasional provinciality. Yet the Massachusetts Bay colonists had no intention of cutting themselves off from England. They were English, and they looked to England not with sentimental nostalgia but with genuine concern. Many thought of America as only a temporary haven, and a goodly number of colonists did in fact return to England when the Church of England lost its episcopal hierarchy.[2]

The founders of the Massachusetts Bay Colony intended, as John Winthrop said on the voyage to America, "by a mutual consent through a special overruling providence and a more than ordinary approbation of the churches of Christ to seek out a place of cohabitation and consortship under a due form of government both civil and ecclesiastical." Because they judged themselves to be a select company, selected by God, and because they were entering a new land, they could sense what God intended them to be. The Massachusetts Bay colonists were instructed by Winthrop to think of themselves "as a city upon a hill; the eyes of all people are upon us."[3]

The essence of the due form of ecclesiastical government that they adopted, congregationalism, is what Winthrop called "a mutual consent," the idea of the covenant. A Congregational church consists of a covenanting group of believers who acknowledge their faith to one another. Such a covenant was adopted by a group within Cotton's Lincolnshire church, so that congregationalism existed within the episcopal system. This scheme of things was not intended by Cotton and the other covenantors to be a separation from the Church of England, for Separatists were thought to be schismatists and radicals. Separatism meant a break with the past as fundamental as had been the separation from Rome; and, since Cotton and most other Puritans believed that grace had come to them through the ministry of the Anglican Church, to separate from it seemed blasphemous. Separation had serious practical disadvantages as well. But when these non-Separatist Puritans came to America, they did in fact separate themselves from the Church of England, its government, and its system of ordaining ministers, even though the descendants of the Puritans down into the eighteenth century denied that they had separated themselves and argued that they were still members of the Church of England. Because they claimed they had not separated, they could take the position that their churches were in New England what the Church of England was in the old country, the one authorized church. Had they admitted that they had separated, others not of their ecclesiastical persuasion might have judged that they could organize rival churches.

The Background of Cotton's Defenses

The central notion of congregationalism is that a church consists of a group of committed Christians who have joined together for their mutual edification and for the performance of their duties toward God. As has been noted, Cotton had managed to bring together such a group within St. Botolph's Church: people to whom he could, in his judgment, properly offer the Sacrament of the Lord's Supper. Like other Puritans, Cotton was interested in discipline: he did not want to administer the Lord's Supper to the unworthy. This concern was to be a continuing one for Cotton.[4] It can hardly be said that Cotton's group of covenantors had all the characteristics of full-blown congregationalism. Specifically, the St. Botolphers did not elect their own minister.

Well before John Cotton came to America in 1633, the first Massachusetts Bay Congregational churches were established. In 1629, thirty colonists in Salem joined in a covenant, elected two men who had been Church of England ministers to the offices of teacher and pastor, and then ordained the two by the laying on of hands.[5] The next year, when John Winthrop, the newly elected governor of Massachusetts Bay, arrived in Salem as leader of a substantial body of colonists, he and other leaders sought to receive the Lord's

Supper but were denied. The Salem ministers also refused to baptize a child born at sea. Back in England, John Cotton heard of these events and protested. He argued: "Two things . . . I conceive to be erroneous, first, that you think no man may be admitted to the Sacrament though a member of the catholic church unless he be a member of some particular reformed church. Secondly, that none of our congregations in England are particular reformed churches but Mr. Lathrop's and such as his. . . . This explicit and solemn covenant is rather a solemn vow to bind the members of the church together in nearer fellowship with God and one another than any such essential cause without which it cannot be."[6] (John Lathrop was a proto-Congregationalist, minister to a London church.)[7] Clearly Cotton had not fully developed his ideas about the nature of a "visible church" in 1630.

In 1633, when Cotton was on his way to America, his wife bore a child. Cotton did not elect to have his son, who was born at sea, baptized until he had himself joined a church, "1. because they had no settled congregation [at sea]; 2. because a minister hath no power to give the seals but in his own congregation."[8] Cotton had become a Congregationalist.

Cotton went to a Congregational colony; there he joined a church that had been "gathered," according to Congregational terminology, within a month of the arrival of its members. He was enthusiastically installed as teacher of the Boston church. The Boston church's covenant, which one was required to accept in order to be a church member, reads: "I do promise, by the grace and help of the Lord Jesus, that I will forsake all my former lusts and corruptions, wherein at any time I have walked, and that I will give myself to the Lord Jesus, making him my only priest and atonement, my only prophet and guide, my only king and law giver, and that I will yield subjection to him in this church, and all his ordinances herein according to the Gospel, and will walk with this church in mutual memberly love and succor, according to God."[9]

New Boston, the town in which Cotton settled, was located on a peninsula two miles long and a mile wide, almost an island, since the neck that connected it to the mainland was sometimes underwater. In 1633, when Cotton arrived, there were only about forty houses. By the end of the year, the population of the town was only about four hundred—men, women, and children, including servants. Cotton attracted some well-to-do families to Boston, but during the 1630s the town's meetinghouse was small and windowless, with walls of clay and a thatched roof.[10] It could hardly be said to resemble the church to which Cotton had ministered for some twenty years, the beautiful St. Botolph's Church.

Cotton's acceptance of the already-established system might in fact have been reluctant had he not feared a movement toward separatism through the work of the extremist Roger Williams, who was demanding such a complete break with the past that members of Congregational churches would have been forbidden to hear sermons by those who were not Congregationalists. Cotton's dealings with Roger Williams in the next decade and his problems with Anne Hutchinson, both discussed elsewhere in this study, affected Cotton's career as a Congregationalist. Williams's banishment in the winter of 1635–1636 led to the extensive debate between Williams and Cotton, and, in the course of it, Congregational Massachusetts was shown to be an enemy of toleration. A consequence of Williams's attack and of events in England was, as Raymond P. Stearns observes, that "whereas in 1641 the Bible Commonwealth was looked upon as an experiment in ecclesiastical liberalism, by 1645 it had become a stronghold of conservatism."[11] Cotton's part in the Anne Hutchinson episode became grounds for attacks on his orthodoxy, and arguments ad hominem became part of the attack on congregationalism.

Four years after Cotton left England, events began to occur that did much to isolate the New Englanders from their old home, though at first the incidents appeared propitious. In 1637, the efforts of Charles I and Archbishop Laud to force a Book of Common Prayer on the Scottish Church resulted in the expensive Bishops' Wars and in a need on the part of Charles for additional funds. When Charles, seeking funds, called a parliament, it was more interested in airing grievances that had accumulated since the previous parliament, eleven long years before. Charles soon dissolved it. Convocation, the assembly of leaders of the Church of England, meeting simultaneously, intensified the current bad feelings by promulgating seventeen new canons, nearly all offensive to the Puritans.

The year 1641 saw another parliament, again called to raise funds for the needy Charles. But, instead, the Long Parliament voted to impeach the Puritans' chief opponent in the Church of England, Archbishop Laud, and it also considered eliminating episcopacy from the church. Those who most resented episcopacy were parish ministers, who wanted for themselves the powers that the bishops were enjoying. Spokesmen for a change, including John Milton, quickly explained the need for the elimination of the "prelates" and for the substitution of presbyteries. When the Long Parliament ordered the establishment of the Westminster Assembly, a mammoth committee of English clergy and Scottish commissioners was appointed to look into the matter; and the Puritans hoped that soon a substitute for episcopacy would be established. The problem facing the clergy at Westminster has been brilliantly diagnosed by William Haller:

The majority of the divines in the assembly, under the urging of the Scots, were proposing that the disciplinary power of the church and the all-important authority to ordain ministers and license preachers be vested in the presbytery or "classis" made up of representatives from the various parishes of a given district. . . . But they were forgetting that they had risen to their present position through the opportunities formerly allowed them to enlist the support of converts and followers regardless of parish boundaries and independent of official central authority. Every Puritan group which at any time joined together to engage a lecturer tended to become a "gathered church" centered in its preaching minister and self-limited in membership to his convinced personal followers.[12]

With Charles engaged in fighting Parliament in the First Civil War, debate in the Westminster Assembly between Presbyterians and Congregationalists delayed a decision as to what polity would be recommended; no decision could effectively be made until the issue of the war had been settled. Americans, including Cotton, entered the debate through their books to propose the establishment of the New England Way in England. But English Congregationalists, quite unlike the Americans, sought toleration for themselves and then, to gain political supporters, toleration for others. Thereafter, the term *Independents* was used for the coalition of sects with which the Congregationalists had identified themselves. Now a conservative force, the Presbyterians strongly opposed the sects—many of which had left Protestant orthodoxy—and attacked the Congregationalists for encouraging the schism the latter were providing.

Though the debate ended with the victory of the Presbyterians, it meant little, for the army opposing Charles had gained more and more political power, and it was identified with the Independents. Oliver Cromwell's soldiers saw the Congregational form of government as a means of freeing them from external religious restrictions. Now the Church of England was theoretically Presbyterian, but all other Protestant groups, save the Episcopalians, were permitted to organize churches on a voluntary basis, and the Presbyterians lacked influence and—what they most desired—power to discipline.

Cotton's efforts to promote congregationalism of the intolerant New England variety bore a poor harvest indeed. Though the few fruits were repulsive to him, it was difficult in remote Massachusetts to understand what made Presbyterians so unhappy with congregationalism. Cotton did come to recognize that, compared with the Independents, the Presbyterians might not be so evil after all; at least the Presbyterians had not embraced toleration. Perhaps Cotton was fortunate not to live until the chaos caused by the saints-in-arms led to the restoration of episcopacy in 1660.

The True Constitution

In 1633, when Cotton became teacher of the church of Boston, an observer with foresight might have predicted that a scholar like Cotton in a town with such great potential would be an important personage in the colony. Within a year, Cotton had begun to draw up a defense of the congregationalism established in Massachusetts Bay, but the time when it was needed to further the cause of congregationalism in England did not come until 1642. Then it was published as *The True Constitution Of A particular visible Church, proved by Scripture*. No works describing the New England Way had been published before, because of censorship and because it would have been unwise to advertise the American practices to the episcopal hierarchy. Now Cotton provided both description and defense, and, although he later prepared more detailed statements, this is an important one because of its early date. It went through four editions. (I cite the third, published in 1644 as *The Doctrine of the Church, To which is committed the Keyes of the Kingdome of Heaven*.)

A church begins with Christians, Cotton teaches. The members of a church rightly organized are those called to salvation by God; they form a church by confessing their sins to one another, professing their faith, and binding themselves by a covenant. The members choose officers, consisting of a pastor, who exhorts the members and dispenses wisdom; a teacher, who dispenses knowledge; and ruling elders, who assist the pastor and the teacher by admitting new members, excommunicating those who should not be members, and seeing to it that "none in the church live either inordinately without a calling or idly in their calling" (3). The elders also prevent and heal offenses in morals and doctrine, prepare matters for congregational consideration, admonish, and visit the sick. Cotton cites Scripture to support all of his organizational plan.

The proper worship service in a Christian church consists of ten activities: (a) prayer; (b) singing of psalms; (c) reading of the Bible (the Word); (d) preaching the Word by giving the sense of it and applying it for the use of the congregation; (e) "where there be more prophets . . . they may prophesy [preach] two or three, if the time permit"; (f) the asking of questions of the preachers (a privilege not available to women); (g) baptism of believers and their children; (h) the Lord's Supper; (i) taking the collection; and (j) the blessing. All churches are equal and independent. If, however, a church offends in doctrine, other churches may admonish it to mend its ways. If the admonition is not heeded, other churches may condemn it and withdraw from fellowship.

Though historically important, this short, clear work has no literary pretensions, and it lacks a sense of the moment in history when it was written. It uses the simple question-and-answer form. It says nothing of the development of the system of congregationalism.

A Sermon . . . Deliver'd at Salem, 1636

More important for students of Cotton and congregationalism is *A Sermon . . . Deliver'd at Salem, 1636,* which finally found its way into print in Boston in 1713.[13] The sermon is prefaced by a retraction in which Cotton tells how, while still in England, he had protested to the pastor of the Salem congregation when magistrates arriving in America were not permitted to receive Communion or have a child baptized. "You went hence," Cotton had written, "of another judgment, and I am afraid your change hath sprung from New Plymouth men."[14] The influence of Plymouth on Massachusetts Bay congregationalism through Deacon Fuller is still being debated. Cotton's own statement here suggests a strong influence,[15] but later he emphasized the continuity of the Congregational tradition from the preemigration period.

Before Cotton had come to America, Roger Williams had been offered the position of teacher by the Boston church. He refused because the church had not separated from the Church of England. After serving briefly in Salem, Williams moved on to the Separatist Plymouth colony, but later he returned to Salem and a position with the church there, though the authorities of the colony disapproved of his teaching. He had some success in Salem persuading the church to adopt a Separatist position before he left again, this time for Narragansett Bay. Because of the tension that had developed between Salem and the colonial authorities, Cotton went to Salem to make peace—and to suggest the dangers of separatism.

In his sermon, Cotton explains that after his criticism of Skelton, he had made a diligent search of the Scriptures that had shown him he was wrong. He had learned that the covenant and its gifts, such as the sacraments, belong not to all believers but only to the seed of Abraham. Thus, just as the Old Testament required that the faithful should join the family of Abraham, the New Testament equivalent is joining a congregation. Cotton had learned too, he reports, that a minister has no power unless he is called by a people; his power, then, is limited in that it extends only to those who have called him. Just as no one can be excommunicated but those who have been admitted to Communion, only those who are possible subjects of excommunication— that is, church members—can be admitted to Communion.

The sermon that follows this address explains in some detail the theology of the covenant, which, significantly, Cotton expounded at this time, just before the beginning of the Anne Hutchinson controversy. This theology, accepted by most Puritans whether or not they were Congregationalists, has been considered by some scholars to be a factor that mitigated the arbitrariness of the Calvinist God and that permitted preachers to teach that people have the power to do much toward their own salvation. In fact, this sermon teaches nothing like voluntarism.

Cotton, like other covenant theologians, conceives of two covenants: the Old, or the Covenant of Works; and the New, or the Covenant of Grace. The first of these God made with Abraham; by it he promised life to those who give exact obedience to his laws, statutes, and judgments. By it, people agree to be cursed of God if they break the covenant by violating the commandments. The second covenant was made with "the people of Israel and Judah . . . especially after their return from Babel and yet more especially under the days of the New Testament" (46). By this covenant God promises his people Christ and everlasting communion with him in return for faith in Christ, the obedience of faith (the righteousness such as only those given grace can have), and repentance. That this second covenant is a perpetual one, Cotton teaches, shows the necessity for a church covenant:

> The use of this point . . . may show us . . . a ground of that which some of us (yet but few) saw the truth of, in our native country, namely the necessity of a church covenant to the institution of a church. "Come, and let us join ourselves to the Lord." That which doth make a people a joined people with God, that doth make a church. What is that? The Covenant of Grace doth make a people a joined people with God and therefore a church of God, and therefore you shall find that when the Lord establishes Israel for a church unto Himself, He maketh this covenant. (55)

The covenant is thus a theological notion as well as an ecclesiastical one.

The real issue was the one that Cotton next addressed. If a Christian should properly join a particular church, then should he not refuse association with members of the Church of England, which failed to recognize that true churches are formed by covenant? Cotton answers with a whole series of arguments, then concludes: "I am marvellously afraid of separation from churches upon any breach of duty. They who do separate for such causes, think they are sprinkled with the water of separation: but believe it, they are separated from Christ Jesus forever, if they so live and so die. Therefore if you belong to Christ, He will show you it is not the water of separation that will serve your turn but getting Christ Jesus, and sitting close to Him and to your brethren, by admonishing and reproving them if you see them defiled" (68). Unlike the Covenant of Works, the Covenant of Grace, Cotton teaches, is not conditional.

Letter to Lord Say and Seal

In New England the covenant was political too. Since the requisite for membership in a church was faith, and since God gives sanctifying grace to those who have faith, the best rulers, according to Massachusetts thinking, ought then to be church members. To an English nobleman who contemplated settling in Massachusetts, Lord Say and Seal, this scheme did not look attractive. Cotton justified the Massachusetts policy in a letter written in 1636. It was not published until 1764, when it appeared in Thomas Hutchinson's *History of Massachusetts Bay.*

Cotton believed that, although the churches and the state should be intimately related, they should also be separate. The state should be organized according to the pattern that he believed God described in the Bible so that the churches could be vigorous. The state exists, in part, for the sake of the church. Though Cotton believed that God had described the ideal political order, he thought that God left room for human discretion. Democracy, often identified with congregationalism in the history of ideas, was not, according to Cotton, an available option: "Democracy I do not conceive that ever God did ordain as a fit government either for church or commonwealth. If the people be governors, who shall be governed? As for monarchy and aristocracy, they are both of them clearly approved and directed in Scripture, yet so as referreth the sovereignty to Himself, and [God] setteth up theocracy in both as the best form of government in the commonwealth as well as in the church." But theocracy did not mean that the ministers were to rule. God ruled, through his saints. The fact that church members chose the leaders, Cotton protested, did not mean that the form of government was democratic, for democracy is government by the people, not by the governors. It is right for the church to choose members as governors, he maintained, for the church has the function in Massachusetts of preparing "fit instruments both to rule and to choose rulers."[16]

The fact that the people, or rather those church members who chose the responsibility of serving as "freemen," were given political power was itself a consequence of covenant theory. Edmund S. Morgan notes that, according to Massachusetts Bay political theory, the government did not derive its power from the people, yet the establishment of government depended on a voluntary covenant made by the people. The officials who administered the government were chosen by the freemen but empowered by God. This covenant theory of government was part of the European movement that led to the conception of all social relationships as contractual ones.[17]

A year after Cotton's correspondence with Lord Say and Seal, another questioning letter arrived. This time, thirteen English ministers wrote to the New England clergy to question them about their church practices. They were distressed at reports that the American churches held that a set form of prayer and the use of the liturgy were unlawful; that the Lord's Supper was forbidden to those not members of a Congregational church; that baptism was administered only to the children of church members; and that the chief power of the churches was in the hands of members. Cotton promised to send an explanation of the situation, and the following year he did present the defense of Massachusetts's rejection of set forms of prayer discussed in an earlier chapter. No full answer to the other questions was sent till 1639, when John Davenport answered. Both the original letter and Davenport's reply were published in Simeon Ash and William Rathband's *A Letter of Many Ministers in Old England* (London, 1643); Cotton's letter is in the Cotton Papers in the Prince Collection of Boston Public Library.

A Coppy of a Letter

Several years before his extended defenses of the New England Way were published, another letter that Cotton wrote to a correspondent in England found its way into print. In this letter, published as *A Coppy of a Letter* (1641), Cotton assured his correspondent that prospective church members (a) were required neither to disclaim the churches of which they had formerly been members nor to profess repentance for their former communion with English churches and (b) did not covenant never to have communion with the English churches. Cotton noted that the principal cause for excommunication from the Massachusetts churches had been the rejection of communion with the English churches: "What you speak of separatists and Brownists we generally here do consent with you that the bitterness of separation whereby men do not only cut themselves from the inventions of men but also from the ordinances of God and fellowship of his servants, for who so have done, they never were blessed with peace."[18] Such a separation had been demanded by Roger Williams, who wanted the new churches to cut themselves off from what he considered to be the corruption of the English churches. It is interesting to note that a correspondent of Governor Winthrop wrote: "Your disclaiming of Mr. Williams' opinions and your dealings with him so as we hear you did took off much prejudice from you with us."[19] Cotton's disclaimer was published just two years before Williams began his attack on Cotton on the issue of toleration.

A Coppy of a Letter demonstrates the importance for the Massachusetts Bay colonists of maintaining the fiction that their churches were part of the Church of England. Since the government of the colony was authorized by the English Crown so that its power could be said to be legitimate, the colonists could, in Perry Miller's words, "call any church they established part of the Church of England, and, therefore, by grace of magistrates of their own creating, could enforce complete obedience to it." Thus they could "transport both the English State and Church to Massachusetts and there reform them at will."[20]

The Way of the Churches

The full description of the New England Way that Cotton had promised was prepared in the early 1640s. Entitled *The Way of the Churches of Christ in New-England,* the work circulated in manuscript for some time, according to the prefatory epistle, which complains of the difficulty of obtaining the authorities' permission to have such Congregationalist works published. The authors of this prefatory epistle consider *The Way* as supplemental to *The Keyes of the Kingdom of Heaven,* published the year before; Cotton later complained that *The Way* should not have been published, as it represented a position that he no longer held. The variations from Cotton's position in the authoritative *Keyes* seem slight; the chief one is the important question of the power of the elders, which—as we have seen—was considered to be crucial by the English Congregationalists. In *The Way* Cotton emphasizes somewhat less the power of the elders and somewhat more the power of the congregation. The work would thus have been less appealing to a power-seeking member of the English clergy. The English who published *The Way* considered it to contain basically their position, on the virtues of which, they believed, it shed new light. *Keyes* had a peculiar importance because it explained the authority by which the New England Way had been established; today *The Way* seems far more attractive and interesting.

The Way of the Churches, a work twice the length of *The Keyes,* describes some of the theory of congregationalism but is in the main a description of Congregational practice in New England. Cotton emphasizes the importance of religion in New England when he reports that those who go there and desire to join a church profess "that it was the principal end of their coming, to enjoy the presence of the Lord in the liberty and purity of His ordinances" (6). Sometimes newcomers come in a group, and the group (like Thomas Hooker's) is "loath to part company and yet so great that they cannot well join in any one church already established without too much impeachment of their outward estate and livelihood, the chiefest part of the lands belonging to each church being prepossessed by others before them." They then may decide to form a new church, in which case they "inquire out someone or other of eminent gifts, usually such as have been preachers of good esteem in England, who may guide and go along with them in so great an action" (6–7).

In New England the next step is to tell the governor and some of the local magistrates of the intention to form a church, and to invite their representatives and those of nearby churches to meet with them on the day of their church gathering. (In fact, the General Court in 1636 had ordered that no church was to be gathered without the prior consent of the majority of elders and magistrates of the colony.)[21] On the appointed day, a spokesman for the members of the church being gathered professes on their behalf repentance and faith, propounds the "covenant of promise," denies any ability in themselves to keep the covenant, and declares "their acceptance of the Lord for their God, and the Lord Jesus (the head and Savior of His church) to be their king, priest, and prophet, and give up themselves in professed subjection unto all His holy ordinances" (8).

Much of *The Way of the Churches* is devoted to a discussion of the proper officers of a church, their responsibilities, qualifications, and method of selection. A point of particular concern to Cotton is the role of the ruling elder, as distinguished from that of the preaching elder. The ruling elder is not a layman, Cotton insists, but is ordained and has important powers, particularly in connection with admitting new members and maintaining high moral standards in the community. (Ironically, the position of the ruling elder was abandoned after the first generation in New England.)

It is to the ruling elders that a candidate for church membership applies. They examine the applicant's knowledge of religious principles, his experience with grace, and his moral behavior ("his godly conversation among men"). If he is acceptable to the ruling elders, they tell the church. If the members believe him to be worthy, the applicant publicly confesses his sins, explains how God's grace drew him out of his sins and into fellowship with Christ, declares that he has "good knowledge of the principles of religion," professes his subjection to the Gospel and his desire to walk in it "with the fellowship of that church" (55). After testimonials are offered in his behalf, he accepts the church covenant and is a member.

It is unfortunate that Cotton did not describe the implications of walking "with the fellowship of that church." One of his parishioners, Robert Keayne, kept a notebook on the proceedings of Cotton's church; and the notebook, still extant, gives us a surprisingly attractive picture of the fellowship. On the basis of his study of the notebook, Larzer Ziff calls it "a deeply felt relationship" that gave "a sense of social solidarity" to the members.[22]

The Way is an answer to Cotton's critics (unnamed) as well as a description of American practices. The explanation of how the churches admit members is followed by a defense of three Congregational practices: that only those possessing "gracious qualification" are admitted as members, that members are received by covenant, and that power is given to the people in the admission of members. The first practice, as we shall see, is defended at length elsewhere in Cotton's works; the second and third defenses reveal much about Cotton's habits of mind and predispositions.

Early in *The Way* Cotton upholds the covenant as an Old Testament institution and asserts that it is "evident by the light of nature that all civil relations are founded in covenant." Here he uses the same familiar arguments, adding that in the New Testament the church members at Ephesus are referred to as fellow citizens with the saints, and the word *citizens* implies a covenant since all civil citizenship is based on a covenantal relationship. Since Cotton elsewhere rejects the testimony of the light of nature in determining religious questions (it is vain imaginings), this argument is not very persuasive. The Old Testament argument is indeed consistent with Cotton's basic assumption that laws made in the Old Testament apply in New Testament times unless Christ specifically abrogated them. Still, Cotton is uneasy about the lack of a clear description of a church covenant in the New Testament: "in the days of the New Testament, the magistrates and princes of the earth being aliens and enemies to the church, the apostles thought it meet to speak of this covenant not plainly but as it were in parables and similitudes" (62). (An influential Congregationalist of a later generation, Solomon Stoddard, protested, "There is no syllable in the Word of God intimating any such thing" as a church covenant.)[23]

Again when Cotton defends the Congregational practice of admitting new members by the consent of the old ones, he recognizes that it may sound dangerously like democracy for the people to have so much power; but he protests that he is compelled to accept the principle since Christ gave the power of the keys to the church. Cotton's lack of sympathy for the position he presents makes his attempt at justification less persuasive.

One of the most difficult tasks that Cotton had to undertake was to explain why members of the Church of England were not permitted to receive the Lord's Supper in New England churches even though members of other Congregational churches were admitted. The difficulty with the distinction is that it made clear the actual separation that existed between the Church of

England and the American churches—a separation that Cotton and his colleagues were trying to deny. It is perhaps this portion of the book, as well as Cotton's discussion of the power of the church members, that made him regret publication of the work.

Members from other New England churches were permitted, Cotton explains, to receive the Lord's Supper if they brought a letter of recommendation from the church of which they were members or if their churches had made known their desire to have their visiting members received. But those who were members of the Church of England and had left their home parish were not members of a particular church, nor did they bring letters of recommendation. In addition, they came from churches that were defiled with five public offenses, which they had first specifically to repent: they belonged to a national and therefore unscriptural church (earlier Cotton denied this was a sin), they came to the Lord's table without public profession of repentance and faith; they came to the Lord's table with ignorant and scandalous persons; they worshiped God with the inventions of men; and they accepted an unscriptural form of church government. (In *A Coppy of a Letter* [1641] Cotton had denied that new members were required to make such confessions.)

As a whole, *The Way* reveals Cotton as a confident proponent of congregationalism, though he had difficulty with certain objections to it. He makes clear that he considered New England churches to be the model that English churches should follow, and his extensive criticisms of the most puritanical of the English churches in the closing pages of the book demonstrate no awareness that New England congregationalism was not to find acceptance in England.

The Keyes of the Kingdom of Heaven

In 1642, the year following the publication of *A Coppy of a Letter,* Lord Say and Seal, who had not after all emigrated, and several other members of Parliament wrote to Cotton as the leading Massachusetts Bay minister and also to Thomas Hooker and John Davenport, the leading ministers of Connecticut and New Haven, urging them to return to England, where they were needed as members of the Westminster Assembly. None of the three attended, but Cotton wrote a book to persuade the assembly to adopt for England the Congregational way. This work, *The Keyes of the Kingdom of Heaven* (1644), was endorsed by the two leading members of Cotton's ecclesiastical party in England, Thomas Goodwin and Philip Nye. *Keyes* was important because of its approach and because of the high regard for Cotton among

Puritans. His opponent Thomas Edwards called him "the greatest divine," the "prime man of them all in New England."[24]

Keyes would be more interesting were it a description of what was going on in the Massachusetts churches, instead of being a statement of Cotton's conception of the authority and power of the church as they are presented in Scripture. That the book went through seven printings suggests that it was widely read. Its historical importance is suggested by the fact that the leading English Presbyterians wrote books in answer.

The Keyes of the Kingdom of Heaven is presented as an explanation of Matthew 16:19: "And I give unto thee the keys of the kingdom of heaven, and whatsoever thou shalt bind on earth shall be bound in heaven, and whatsoever thou shalt loose on earth shall be loosed in heaven." The keys were given, according to Cotton, not only to Peter, to whom Christ spoke, but to all the apostles, or rather to each of the apostles separately. The power that they received went, in turn, to all of the church. Now, as a result, when a group of Christians gather together to form a church, they possess as a church the power of the keys given to Peter and the apostles. Thus the basic unit of the Christian church is the individual congregation, and it is from this unit that all ecclesiastical power is derived. For example, "the complete integrity of a minister's calling" rests on the power given him by his people (37).

What is this power, the power of the keys? According to Cotton, it is, first, faith, the faith common to all believers. Second, it is the power to enter the fellowship of a church, to choose gifted men as officers, to partake of the sacraments, and to censure offenders. The officers are given powers of various kinds by those who choose them. Elders have power to preach, to call the church together, to judge and pronounce sentences on offenders before the church, to separate the true disciples from the rest of the people if the latter fall away from Christ, and to perform certain other admonitory and administrative functions.

These are the basic powers given by Christ to his church, according to Cotton. There is no transcendent power given to an official such as a diocesan bishop. Beyond the individual congregation there is, however, the synod, where elders may meet to treat three kinds of problems. First, the synod may help provide peace or light for a church that seeks it, as did the church at Antioch; second, it may reprove a church that is corrupt in doctrine, when private reproof has failed; and third, it may try to effect a general reformation when the churches seem to be growing corrupt. The synod may not enjoin what is by nature indifferent (what Scripture neither requires nor forbids); it may not legislate but may see that the laws that Christ made are published and observed.

The power of the synod was the question that most separated Presbyterians and Congregationalists, but closely related to it was the relationship of the members of the separate churches to one another. Presumably because his English brethren had not looked with pleasure upon the lack of friendly relationships among members of different congregations, Cotton in *The Keyes* modified the position he had set forth in the address that preceded his Salem sermon of 1636. He now taught that one of the liberties given by Christ was communion with other churches, not only through the synods that could be formed but also by members of a church receiving the Lord's Supper in other churches. A church might work with other congregations by keeping an eye on visiting church members, by recommending a church member who moved to the neighborhood of another church, by giving and receiving supplies, and by propagating the faith through missionaries. Cotton also defines the proper relationship of church and state. The church does not derive power from the state but is subject to it, for the state has power to enforce civil peace. Civil peace required "the establishment of pure religion in doctrine, worship, and government according to the Word of God, as also the reformation of all corruptions in any of these" (50).

As developed in practice, this arrangement did as much to prevent the spread of heresy and toleration as the discipline of Presbyterian synods could have done, but to Presbyterians it must have sounded like the despised Erastianism developing in England. In Massachusetts, magistrates claimed jurisdiction over offenses against the first four of the Ten Commandments, and the General Court of Massachusetts drew up in time a code that required punishment by the state for such heresies as denying the resurrection of the body.[25]

The Keyes of the Kingdom of Heaven is written in a most cautious, unpolemical tone. It was intended to serve the cause of moderation, or so at least said those who arranged its publication. In a preface to the book, the English Congregationalists describe the New England Way as a middle way between Brownism or separatism, which reduces the power of the elders by putting church government into the hands of the people, and Presbyterianism, which reduces the power of the individual elder in his church by putting church government into the hands of a district presbytery. For Cotton's English colleagues, the publication of an American work such as *Keyes* had two advantages over the publication of their own efforts, such as *An Apologeticall Narration*. First, it had experience behind it and therefore seemed more authoritative than their own pronouncements. Second, since it was not their own statement that they were issuing, they were less subject to attack for it by the Presbyterians.

The Way of Congregational Churches Cleared

Although Congregational theory dates from the early years of the seventeen century, most English Puritans had not looked hard at questions of ecclesiastical polity since the days of Thomas Cartwright's early efforts in the 1570s and 1580s. Minor reforms, such as those requested of James I in 1604, were all that most Puritans dared hope for until the events of the 1640s. Then the advocates of reform were largely Scots, who sought for England the kind of ecclesiastical government that they knew in Scotland. Among these were Robert Baillie, who took out on John Cotton some of the frustrations that he was experiencing at the Westminster Assembly. Baillie attacked Cotton in *A Dissuasive from the Errours of the Time* (1645). Here Baillie identified Cotton and his ecclesiastical position with that of separatism and Brownism; and he then identified Brownism with Anabaptism, which most Protestants regarded as the worst kind of radicalism and anarchism. Cotton's reply, *The Way of Congregational Churches Cleared,* not published until 1648, is one of his most interesting works because much of it is autobiographical. Cotton was defending himself and his cause at a time he knew to be crucial. He intended it for the press, but doubtless he was unhappy that the author of the prefatory epistle saw the treatise not as a defense of the church polity that ought to be adopted but as a means of demonstrating to the Presbyterians that the Congregationalists deserved to be accepted in church fellowship. Cotton's delay in answering his Presbyterian opponents with this work may well have been caused by his taking time the previous year to answer the attacks of Roger Williams. Now he had to reply to criticisms of his treatment of the Anne Hutchinson affair.

Cotton begins *The Way . . . Cleared* with a description of the origins of modern congregationalism, the term that appears to be Cotton's invention and that he preferred to the common English term *"Independency,"* since the latter was used by other groups, such as the Baptists, the Seekers, and the Familists. For Cotton, the most important Separatist was not Robert Browne, founder of the Brownists, or Henry Barrow, founder of the Barrowists, but John Robinson, pastor of the Plymouth Pilgrims when they were residing in Holland. Robinson was a Separatist, and, though he became only a moderate one, Cotton could not approve of him but notes that the further reformation of the Church of England that Parliament and the Westminster Assembly had been making eliminated from the Church those features which had led to Robinson's separation.

Following the preliminary defense against the charge of separatism from the attacks of Baillie, Cotton next considers in a very important passage the history of his own group. This passage, which is often cited because in it Cotton presents the "roots" of the New England Way, is worth quoting at length:

That the separatists were our fathers, we have justly denied . . . seeing that they neither begat us to God, nor to the church, nor to their schism. That we are (through grace) begotten to God and to His church, we received (many of us) from the blessing of Christ upon the ministry of England. That we grew weary of the burden of episcopacy and conformity, we received from the Word of God by the help of the non-conformists there. That we laid aside the Book of Common Prayer, we received from the serious meditation of the Second Commandment, and not from the writings of the separatists, though they also had taken up the same conclusion upon other premises. The particular visible church of a congregation to be the first subject of the power of the keys, we received by the light of the Word from Mr. Parker, Mr. Baynes, and Dr. Ames, from whom also (from two of them at least) we received light out of the Word for the matter of the visible church to be visible saints, and for the form of it to be a mutual covenant, whether an explicit or implicit profession of faith and subjection to the Gospel of Christ in the society of the church or presbytery thereof. . . . And having received these, not from the separatists but from the Lord Jesus, by gracious saints and faithful witnesses of Jesus, the consanguinity of our tenents with any the like found amongst the separatists will not demonstrate the separatists to be our fathers. (13)

Cotton thus identifies his tradition as being non-Separatist. He does admit, however, that the Massachusetts Bay Colony practice was influenced by the American Separatist camp at Plymouth: "some of the first comers might help their theory by hearing and discerning their practice at Plymouth" (17). But Cotton tells his opponent that he himself had made a covenant with members of his congregation in Lincolnshire.

The sense of unity that these Congregationalists felt was, as Cotton indicates, a result of their common experiences. Paul Baynes and Robert Parker, both of whom had died in 1617, were prominent, influential Puritans. Preacher at Great St. Andrew's Church in Cambridge from 1602, Baynes must have been well known to Cotton, to Thomas Hooker, and perhaps to John Winthrop, who studied at Cambridge and became a Puritan during Baynes's years there. William Ames (who died in 1633) arranged for the publication of Baynes's important posthumous *The Diocesans Trial* (1621), and he also translated into Latin in 1610 the even more important *English Puritanisme* of William Bradshaw. Thomas Hooker, in turn, edited Ames's last work, *A Fresh Suit against Human Ceremonies* (1633). Nearly all of the New England ministers came to America because they were Congregationalists; what Cotton calls "our tenents" had attracted, in England, Hugh Peter,

John Eliot, John Davenport, and all of the better-known ministers who were Cotton's contemporaries. This story is well told in Perry Miller's *Orthodoxy in Massachusetts* (1933).

William Ames's most important work is *Medulla Sacrae Theologiae;* first published in 1623 and then translated into English, it was published in London in an undated edition, perhaps in 1638, as *The Marrow of Sacred Divinity*. A reading of this work offers convincing proof that Cotton relied very heavily indeed on the light that Ames shed on the Word. In *The Marrow* is to be found almost everything that Cotton taught in his Congregational works, and the language is at times so close as to indicate that Cotton had Ames's book before him when he wrote. Ames insists, for example, that the church Christ instituted is not "national, provincial, or diocesan . . . but it is a parochial church or a church of one congregation." It is Ames who emphasizes the importance of a church covenant, "by which believers bind themselves individually to perform all those duties toward God and toward one another which relate to the purpose of the church and its edification." Ames teaches that a minister's ordination depends on his being called by a congregation, that excommunication requires the approval of the congregation, and that ministers are "either pastors and teachers or ruling elders."[26] Cotton's preachings on synods, sacraments, and discipline precisely reflect what Ames's book proposes. Perhaps Cotton felt that, since Ames had intended to come to America but was stopped by death, it was up to him to say what Ames would have said.

Cotton continues his justification of himself and his career by crediting the coming of the Massachusetts Bay Company for the survival of the Massachusetts Indians, who had been severely weakened by a plague on the arrival of the whites. The Indians had not only survived, Cotton declares; they had been given the opportunity to bear the Christian gospel preached by John Eliot. But the hope of extensive missionary successes that Cotton had expressed when he preached to the departing colonists of 1630 had vanished. Cotton prophesied: until the ruin of Antichrist and the conversion of the Jews, only "some sprinklings and gleanings" of Indians could be converted (78).

A principal charge that Cotton was called to answer is that the Congregational system excluded "many thousand Christians whom they dare not deny to be truly religious of all the privileges of the church" (69). Cotton replies that everyone is allowed to attend all services; only the Lord's Supper is limited to church members. "Is it a dishonor to God," questions Cotton, "that such are withheld from the Lord's Table by whom the name of God is dishonored either through their ignorance or scandal?" (73). The godly are all admitted to some church; only the scandalous and those newly arrived and not yet known are not church members.

Here Cotton was being less than generous to the many who then lived in the Massachusetts Bay Colony but were not church members; these were always a majority, though from the earliest years of the colony the least desirable immigrants had been shipped out of the colony. Cotton was on stronger grounds when he answered the charge that no New England minister preached conversion sermons, by citing the published works of Thomas Shepard and Thomas Hooker. (He did well not to spell out what they had preached: Shepard's popular *The Sincere Convert* is subtitled *Discovering the small number of True Believers, And the great difficulty of Saving Conversion.* Hooker was criticized in print for demanding too much of a person in the conversion process.[27])

What was separating the English Presbyterians and the American Congregationalists appears to have been the question of discipline. The Presbyterians and nearly all of the great Continental Reformed theologians supposed every citizen to be a member of the national church, a system that permitted the church to serve as custodian of the morals of the community. In New England, the state served this function, and the church could be selective. But the New England policy was seen by the Presbyterians as a radical departure from the tradition, and Cotton strongly identified himself with the tradition. Consequently, we can understand why Cotton's defenses seem addressed almost as much to himself as to his opponents.

Cotton describes the relationship of the Congregational practices to the Reformed tradition thus:

Though in the bishops' time we did not forthwith receive all the members of the Church of England into the fellowship of our churches, yet (for ought I know) we are not likely to stand aloof from Presbyterial churches faithfully administered, nor from the testimony which they shall give of their members, that may have occasion to traffic hither, and the like do I conceive of other Reformed churches in other nations of Christendom. Presbyterian churches faithfully administered are not wont to admit a mixed profane multitude to the Lord's Supper (90).

Cotton's technique in this defense seems to be to argue that the relationship of the churches would be no problem were all churches to be as faithfully administered as the New England churches.

But Cotton's chief precedent for the practices of New England congregationalism is the way of the early church. The churches of the apostles, argues Cotton, were Congregational; and, during the first three Christian centuries, the examination of catechumens was so strict that no crimes could be charged against the Christians except their faith. The first departures from the way of the apostles occurred during the third century. Later Cotton would prophesy that the church would soon be "resurrected" and return to its glorious earlier state.

The Way . . . Cleared is almost a formless book, for its arrangement is dictated largely by the order of the arguments that Cotton is answering. It contains, nevertheless, much of Cotton's very best prose, on the whole considerably better than what is found in the sermons. (The prose of his sermons is what his readers recorded.) The gentleness that frequently makes the sermons rather tame is gone; instead, we find a remarkable vigor. One of the better passages is the following:

> For the fruits of Congregational discipline in England, they that walk in that way amongst you might speak far more particularly and largely than I here can do at such a remote distance. But if books and letters and reports do not too much abuse us with false intelligence, the great . . . victories whereby the Lord hath wrought salvation for England in these late wars have been as so many testimonies of the blessing of God upon our way. For the chief instruments which God hath delighted to use herein have been the faith and fidelity, the courage and constancy of Independents. And when I say Independents, I mean not those corrupt sects and heresies which shroud themselves under the vast title of Independency, and in the meantime cast off all church government and churches too, but such as profess the Kingdom of Christ in the government of each holy congregation of saints within themselves. Far be it from me to undervalue the brotherly assistance of the Scottish churches and commonwealth in working so great a deliverance for England. Yea, I account their concurrence a greater matter than assistance in this great work. Their exemplary piety and zeal, their courage and confidence in rising up and standing out against the invasion of episcopal tyranny and superstition did doubtless quicken and encourage England to stand for the like liberty in the like cause and to put forth that zeal which the Lord had kindled in the hearts of many for reformation. And this was more than an assistance, even a guidance. (103)

Controversial prose usually has a short life, but if Cotton is to be remembered for his prose, he should be remembered for passages like this one: emphatic, clear, and rhythmical.

The brief and much less interesting second part of *The Way . . . Cleared* is an answer to Samuel Rutherford, a Scottish divinity professor who had seen the work in manuscript and had published in reply *The Due Right of Presbyteries* (1644), and to Daniel Cawdrey, who had been more pugnacious in his anonymous *Vindiciae Clavium* (1645). Against these two, Cotton cites

Scripture and argues logically to maintain that a church exists by virtue of a covenant—not because it has proper ministers. Cotton lines up his favorite authorities in his support: Augustine, William Whitaker (1548–95), Paul Baynes, Junius (1545–1602), and William Ames.

Preface to *The Answer*

In the same year that Cotton's *The Way of Congregational Churches Cleared* was published, 1648, there appeared two other important American defenses of congregationalism: Thomas Hooker's *Survey of the Summe of Church-Discipline* and John Norton's *Responsio ad totam questionum syllogen a Guilelmo Apollonio propositam*. The former, the longest of the defenses of congregationalism, was written several years earlier; but, lost in transit to England, it had to be reconstructed by Hooker, then near death. Norton's book was addressed to a continental audience; it was translated by Douglas Horton and published in 1958 as *The Answer to the Whole Set of Questions of the Celebrated Mr. William Apollonius*. Prefixed to this work is a letter from old England by the Independents Goodwin, Nye, and Simpson, and a letter from New England by John Cotton.

Cotton's letter is a most revealing document: it explains indirectly the reasons for Cotton's later painful sense of separation from his English colleagues. For nonconformists like himself, Cotton declared, only two choices existed in the England of the early 1630s: to perish in prison or to leave the country. The great Puritan leaders advised the latter, for "by the free preaching of the Word and the actual practice of our church discipline" the colonists could offer a great witness.[28] If this was Cotton's mission, surely the course of English history was a disappointment to him, for not only did the English reject his Congregational practices developed in America, but the advocates of congregationalism in England adopted a policy of toleration, which Cotton abhorred.

The Cambridge Platform

Because by definition congregationalism had no central government, the apologias that Cotton prepared were in no way official. They did not bind the churches of the New England Way, and they had not been adopted as official statements of either policy or procedure. In the mid-1640s, however, circumstances demanded something more official; the consequence was the Cambridge Platform of 1648.

As early as 1643, a clergy conference held in Cambridge had disapproved of some of the Presbyterian features that were developing at Newbury, where the ministers wanted to take away from the church members the right of consultation and assent. Nevertheless, Presbyterianism continued to attract New Englanders, and it was of course dominating the Westminster Assembly. Perhaps from a desire to assert militantly their position, now in serious danger for the first time, some ministers in the spring of 1646 requested the General Court to call a synod. The General Court consequently invited the churches to confer for the "establishing and settling" of the right form of church government and discipline. The invitation reads, in part, as follows:

Inasmuch as times of public peace, which by the mercy of God are vouchsafed to these plantations (but how long the same may continue we do not know) are much more commodious for the effecting of such a work than those troublesome times of war and public disturbances thereby, as the example of our dear native country doth witness at this day . . . and considering withal that, through want of the thing here spoken of, some differences of opinion and practice of one church from another do already appear amongst us . . . it is therefore thought expedient . . . that there be a public assembly of the elders and other messengers of the several churches within this jurisdiction.[29]

The questions of baptism and church membership were singled out as matters especially in need of discussion, for a group of New Englanders were petitioning Parliament for redress against the practices of the New England churches in these matters.

Sessions of the synod began in September 1646, with discussions and, more important, with the appointment of a committee to prepare "a model of church government." Appointed were three ministers, Ralph Partridge, Richard Mather, and John Cotton. The synod then adjourned until 1647. As the meetings proceeded, the power shifted from Presbyterians to Independents in England; and the pressure was removed from the synod to declare itself plainly on the vexing questions of church membership and baptism.

Finally, in 1648 the synod adopted a statement by Richard Mather, who drew heavily on Cotton's writings as well as on his own. The result was the Cambridge Platform, or, as the work was entitled when published the next year, *A Platform of Church Discipline Gathered out of the Word of God and Agreed upon by the Elders and Messengers of the Churches Assembled in the synod at Cambridge in New England*. It was prefaced by an important statement by John Cotton. In time the platform was accepted by most of the churches and by the General Court (the legislative body) of Massachusetts. It is thus an official statement of the New England Way. Though soon in need

of extensive revision, it has been called by Williston Walker in his authoritative *Creeds of Congregationalism* "the most important monument of early
New England Congregationalism."[30] It was reprinted again and again,
thirty-four times in all, the latest as recently as 1943.

As has been said, the platform reflects much of Cotton's teachings on congregationalism. The extent of Mather's borrowing may be suggested by these
parallel passages concerning the relationship of one church to another:

Platform	Keyes of the Kingdom
By way of consultation one with another when we have occasion	By way of consultation, one church hath liberty of communicating with another
to require judgement and counsel of other churches, touching any person or cause wherewith they may be better acquainted than ourselves.	to require their judgment and counsel touching any persons or cause they may be better wherewith aquainted than themselves.
As the church of Antioch consulted with the apostles and elders of the church at Jerusalem, about the question of circumcision of the Gentiles. (Walker, *Creeds of Congregationalism,* 230)	Thus the church of Antioch by their messengers consulted with the church at Jerusalem, touching the necessity of circumcision. (18)

Cotton's preface shows him in his role as diplomat. He professes that the
New England churches are eager for fellowship with the Presbyterians and
have consequently accepted "for substance of doctrine" the Westminster
Confession prepared at the assembly in England. Thereby the New England
churches have proved themselves innocent of heresy, and Cotton hopes that
the Presbyterians will not think them guilty of schism for "a different appre-
hension of the mind of Christ . . . in some few points touching church
order."[31] He begins with great modesty and humility. Cotton then speaks
hopefully of how "the example of such poor outcasts as ourselves" (196) may
help prevent extensive internal squabbles among the English Puritans. He
supposes that English churches might be reluctant for American practices to
be used in England because of three disadvantages that had apparently been
brought to his attention. First, congregationalism would despoil the parish
churches by attracting all of their best members. Second, congregationalism
would provide no means of disciplining nonmembers who were ignorant and
scandalous. Third, it would create divisions among families, for members
would belong to several churches.

These problems Cotton had not dealt with before, for earlier he had advocated the establishment of Congregational churches as the sole churches of England; now he considers them as coexisting with Presbyterian churches. Cotton's answers to these three criticisms seem at first to reveal a far more tolerant spirit than he had shown before in his works. He argues, for example, that it is wrong for members to desert Presbyterian churches because of their government. But he goes on to say that they should remain only "to convince their brethren of their sinful defects and duly wait for their reformation" (198).

Another arrangement that Cotton suggests for getting around the criticism is membership in two churches. In this fashion Congregationalists can "either after or before the public assembly of the parish take an opportunity to gather together for the administration of the sacraments and censures and other church ordinances amongst themselves" (199). (This may have been the arrangement Cotton had created in his church in old Boston.) At any rate, Cotton suggests, if the Presbyterians should lose members to the Congregational churches, "it will never grieve the holy hearts of godly ministers that their hearers should follow after Christ" (199). Thus, though he appears to have a desire for fellowship with the Presbyterians, Cotton in fact cannot imagine a situation in which the Congregationalists do not have some sort of superiority.

The second objection—that of discipline of nonmembers—Cotton treats in an even less satisfactory way, at least for anyone who knows what went on in the Massachusetts of Cotton's day. Cotton thinks that the churches provide discipline for nonmembers, since they are required to attend services and since the ministers and the church members tell them of their failings. The nonmembers listen respectfully, for "they see no hope of enjoying church-fellowship or participation in the sacraments for themselves or their children" unless they win the approval of ministers and members (201).

The third objection—familial division—Cotton can answer with greater ease. Good family relations are encouraged by congregationalism, since one of the qualifications for church membership is the good testimony of one's family and the report that one's family is what it should be.

Cotton's closing effort to create good feelings between Presbyterians and Congregationalists is not likely to be regarded as successful by anyone who has read the casuistry of the early portions of the preface. In many ways the preface of the Cambridge Platform is one of the most disturbing of Cotton's writings. The idealism that seems to permeate his earlier Congregational writings has vanished; he seems now only a die-hard, old-school sectarian.

Of the Holinesse of Church Members

By 1650, toleration was permitted for all the English, but Cotton was still defending congregationalism, partly because his commitment to the church polity that he had done so much to formulate was one of the factors that prevented his returning to England. In the prefatory letter to *Of the Holinesse of Church Members* (1650), addressed to the people of Boston in Lincolnshire, Cotton acknowledges the faithfulness of his former parishioners who had annually remembered his financial needs; but he urges them to recognize that, since his old church admits as members people other than "professed saints," he cannot return as their minister. He cites as well his age (sixty-six) and his American obligations, but he is most concerned with their open policy of church membership. The treatise that follows is Cotton's effort to help them eliminate their error. But it is, as Cotton acknowledges, another volley in the battle between himself and his Scottish Presbyterian opponents Robert Baillie and Samuel Rutherford. The treatise is so sophisticated that one suspects Cotton pretty much forgot his former parishioners in the course of composition.

Cotton was writing at a time when the New England churches had already begun lowering their standards for membership, but he was prepared to insist—and on this point he may well have been addressing his New England colleagues—that there is a point beyond which a church could not go and still remain a true church. It is not enough to demand what all of the Reformed churches demand: the pure Word of God purely preached, sacraments duly administered, discipline maintained according to God's Word, and members externally professing their faith. In addition, Cotton demanded that church members give evidence that they had been effectually called, elected, and justified. In fact, however, Cotton merely interpreted one word more strictly than his fellows in this definition of a true visible church. The word is *duly.* The sacraments are not duly administered, argued Cotton, unless they are administered to the right people. Nor can discipline be said to exist where the wrong people are admitted to the church. The only corrupt persons who can be members are those whose corruption has been recognized and who therefore are about to be cut off. Cotton describes what he conceives to be a typical case:

[S]uppose a man born and baptized in the church, after he be grown . . . do continue grossly and securely ignorant of the principles of religion, I suppose such an one may justly be esteemed unregenerate (for without knowledge the mind cannot be good), and being such he may justly be debarred from the fellowship of the Lord's Table and such other church privileges as be peculiar to confirmed members. Suppose further, that such a person being admonished by the elders and brethren of the church for his gross ignorance do nevertheless still continue in gross ignorance and in neglect of [the] means of instruction, and (as is the wont of such) suppose he be known to neglect family duties, prayer, catechising of his household, examination of their profiting by public ordinances, and shall after admonition for these known defects still continue in his ignorance and negligence, and that after public rebukes for the same before the church, I demand whether such a person may not justly be cast out of the church for his unregeneration and these offensive fruits of it? (57)

Cotton himself was reluctant to undertake the discipline of excommunication; in the years 1634 to 1652, only five members of his church were excommunicated. Excommunication was almost complete ostracism. When Anne Hibbins was excommunicated, Pastor John Wilson pronounced:

I do exclude you not only from the fellowship of the church in all the public ordinances of the same, but also from private fellowship and communion with any servants of God in the church, except only in those relations to your own family: to your husband, children, and servants. And for the greater terror and amazing of you, I do here in the name of Christ Jesus and His church deliver you up to Satan and to his power and working; that you which would not be guided by the counsels of God may be terrified and hampered by the snares and powers of Satan for the destruction of your proud flesh, for the humbling of your soul, that your spirit may be saved in the day of the Lord Jesus if it be His blessed will. And so as an unclean beast I pronounce you an excommunicate person.[32]

Readmission after excommunication was not, however, painfully difficult.

It was on admission rather than excommunication that Cotton focused his attention, and for admission he continued to demand public confession of sins, profession of faith, and declaration of willingness to be subject to Christ.

Certain Queries and *A Defence*

Cotton's last published thoughts on congregationalism are contained in *Certain Queries Tending to Accommodation, and Communion of Presbyterian & Congregational Churches,* a work that he completed just before his death in 1652. Published in 1655 as part of *The Covenant of Grace,* it has its own title page, dated 1654. In the work, Cotton displays a somewhat more liberal attitude toward the relationship of the two kinds of churches, probably because of his continuing disillusionment with English Independents. Here Cotton is prepared to admit that Presbyterian congregations are true churches if they have proper preaching and the truth of the Gospel, if they are "not overgrown with ignorant and scandalous persons" (1), and if the congregations call their ministers. He considers the Presbyterians to be closer to the truth now, but he denies that Presbyterian ministers can be considered true and their sacraments valid unless they become more discriminating as to who is admitted to the Lord's Supper and unless they restrict the power of the elders over churches other than the ones to which they minister. Cotton takes back with one hand what he appeared to give away with the other.

Unexpectedly, Cotton foresees intercommunion between Congregationalists and Presbyterians, for an "error in judgment about discipline is not an heresy against the foundation of Christian religion" (8). This attitude is indeed an about-face for Cotton, to whom church discipline had been quite as important as doctrine. (In *The Bloudy Tenent, Washed* [1647], he had argued that "the matter and form" of the church was a fundamental of religion in the same class with the doctrine of the resurrection of the body.)

Another late work is *A Defence of Mr. John Cotton From the Imputation of Selfe Contradiction,* with a long preface by John Owen. This work, written in answer to Daniel Cawdrey's *Inconsistency of the Independent Way* (1651), shows that seeming inconsistencies between Cotton's *The Way of the Congregational Churches Cleared*, his *The Keyes of the Kingdom of Heaven*, and his *The Way . . . Cleared* and Thomas Hooker's *Survey of the Summe of Church-Discipline* are merely verbal differences. This work has, however, little interest or importance.

Cotton's Congregational works had an authoritative significance in his own time that is difficult to appreciate today. The Puritans' efforts in the 1640s to complete the reformation of the Church of England were the culmination of the work of nearly a hundred years. Through the press, Cotton was the chief spokesman for the Congregational interpretation of the Bible on church government. With toleration the order of the day in England and with the gradual discovery in New England that Cotton's congregationalism was unworkable because the churches were coming to have fewer and fewer members, these writings soon lost their importance. Today their chief value is the light they shed on the first generation of settlers in Massachusetts Bay colony, their ideals and aspirations.

Chapter Five

The Means of Grace:
The American Sermons

However substantial Cotton's reputation was as a preacher in England, he loomed a larger star in America. Benjamin Woodbridge, a Harvard graduate who returned to England to become a preacher of note, called Cotton

> A man of might, at heavenly eloquence,
> To fix the ear and charm the conscience,
> As if Apollos were reviv'd in him,
> Or he had learned of a seraphim.[1]

Although Cotton shared the pulpit of his church in Massachusetts Bay colony with John Wilson, New England practices supplied him with many opportunities to preach. On the Sabbath, Wilson preached in the morning and Cotton in the afternoon, except during Cotton's second year. Then he did all the preaching, for Wilson had returned to England on business. In addition, Cotton preached every other Thursday and on many special occasions, such as at the time of elections.

The Covenant of Grace

Perhaps the earliest of Cotton's extant American sermons are those published under the titles *The New Covenant . . . Being the substance of sundry Sermons* (1654), *The Covenant of Grace* (1655), and *A Treatise of the Covenant of Grace* (1659), all based on the same sermons. A recent commentator refers to these sermons as "great."[2] The first volume was published with Cotton's consent after he had read and corrected it. The third volume was likewise corrected by the author, yet the 1659 edition is a third longer than the first edition. The explanation is that both volumes were compiled from notes. The epistle to the 1659 edition, which I have used, refers to "the diversity of amanuenses, who did take the notes of his sermons, some writing the same more largely and exactly than others." It is difficult to imagine why these sermons, which from their subject matter appear to have been delivered about 1636 (just before the outbreak of the Anne Hutchinson controversy), were not published earlier. The editors, perhaps, thought of this publication as a memorial tribute. The reader is constantly aware of the historical context.

Turning to this volume after reading the several collections of Cotton's English sermons, one notices several differences. First, the sermons seem to have been prepared for a congregation more theologically sophisticated than Cotton's English audiences; there is a precision and care about knotty points of theology not found earlier. Second, Cotton preaches a stricter, more "Calvinistic" theology than he had earlier. But he still dwells on imagery, as noted in the discussion of Cotton's English sermons. Because of the time when they were preached and the great care that they usually show, these are among Cotton's most important sermons.

Cotton's text for all of these sermons is Acts 7:8: "and He gave him the covenant of circumcision, and so Abraham begat Isaac, and circumcised him the eighth day, and Isaac begat Jacob, and Jacob begat the twelve patriarchs." In this passage Cotton finds the idea of the continuing covenant of God and his people, a covenant based not on works, as was the covenant with Adam, but on faith. The central concepts of the covenant of faith, or of grace, have already been considered in chapter 4. But here Cotton makes clearer the relationship of Jesus Christ to the covenant: "God gave Himself to be a God to Abraham and to his seed, and received Abraham and his seed to be a people unto Himself, and the chiefest of this seed, the Lord Jesus Christ, He took to be the mediator or surety of this covenant between them both" (3). The idea of covenant may seem to imply some kind of rational understanding between God and humanity by which God agrees not to be altogether arbitrary in his decisions as to who shall be saved and who shall be damned. Cotton teaches, however, that in the agreement God keeps not only his own part of the contract but also that of the person who is saved. The contract is not conditional but absolute, for God is absolute and has involved himself with both sides of the agreement. In this regard Cotton departed from the teachings of other New England ministers, as we shall see in chapter 6.[3]

To bring a person into the covenant, God takes four steps. First, he separates him from his sins and passions by showing him that they are delivering him to damnation. Second, God shows man that he can have no confidence in his own works. Third, God "taketh up His seat in the soul" (19). Finally, by his spirit God works faith in the soul so that it receives Jesus Christ: "the Spirit of God taking possession in our hearts and working this faith in us, thereby we submit unto the Lord, and this is faith in Jesus Christ, that maketh us one with Christ, for our effectual calling bringeth us to be one with Him" (21).

As Cotton describes the process, it thus has distinct stages; and no one is within the covenant until he has been given faith, the fourth step. For this crucial gift God prepares a person through the previous steps. Later Cotton cautiously adds, "Reserving due honor to such gracious and precious saints as may be otherwise minded, I confess I do not discern that the Lord worketh and giveth any saving preparation in the heart till He give union with Christ [Cotton's fourth step], for if the Lord do any saving qualification before Christ, then the soul may be in the state of salvation before Christ, and that seemeth to be prejudicial unto the grace and truth of Jesus Christ" (39–40). The key phrase here is *saving qualification*, a phrase that suggests that entrance to the Covenant of Grace is conditional. For Cotton there can be no qualifying for grace.

It has been supposed that the "precious saints" to whom Cotton refers include Thomas Hooker, who speaks of preparation as a saving work, and a work of the Spirit."[4] But both Hooker and Cotton teach that God prepares a man for faith and union with Christ, and both also teach that the process is wholly God's, not man's. Hooker does indeed teach that a man who is prepared for Christ and who dies is saved, but he also explains that "when the heart is fitted and prepared, the Lord Christ comes immediately into it."[5]

In his English sermons Cotton maintained that sanctification is good evidence of one's election. At that time he neglected the possibility that, by urging a person to look to his works as evidence that he was justified, the preacher might induce him to seek his salvation by these works rather than by faith. Such a possibility seems to have been brought home to Cotton when he found that his own doctrine of the intimate connection of church and commonwealth was leading the magistrates, whose concern, of course, was civil discipline, to emphasize morality as *the* proof of piety: in Larzer Ziff's words, "to believe that morality argued piety and that without morality there was no piety."[6] Cotton's doctrine that the state should be governed by those gifted with grace, the church members, did indeed emphasize sanctification.

At any rate, in *A Treatise of the Covenant of Grace* Cotton urged his hearers to beware of judging the state of their souls by their power to perform good works. In the Covenant of Works, Cotton warns, God gives a temporary kind of sanctification, so that good works are "no evidence or witness of our union with Christ" (43). To tell the difference between this sanctification and the kind that follows justification is "a matter so narrow that the angels in heaven have much ado to discern who differ" (44). Indeed, Cotton says, "so glorious may this common sanctification be that it may dazzle the eyes of the best of God's children" (54).

The real test, Cotton now urges, is the nature of one's faith: "the true sanctification of a sincere Christian is not discernable until the first discern his justifying faith" (55). This is precisely the position that Cotton took in his dispute with his clerical colleagues in the Anne Hutchinson case. Cotton does not neglect the fact that the doctrine of proof helps prevent any relaxation of effort: those who have a true faith, he teaches, feel the need for greater faith; those who have a temporary faith are confident of their faith.

In his belief that assurance of salvation comes through discerning one's faith, Cotton follows Calvin. In his explanation of the difficulty of distinguishing true sanctification from the sanctification that observance of the Law creates, Cotton follows Perkins. The position Cotton rejects is that of Calvin's successor, Theodore Beza.

Next Cotton raises a vital question. If the salvation process does not require man's cooperation—the Arminian position that Cotton rejects—of what use are the promises? (An example of what Cotton calls the promises is John 3:16, "For God so loved the world that He gave His only begotten Son, that whosoever believeth in Him should not perish but have everlasting life.") These promises instruct, Cotton answers; they show the source of life and salvation. But also—and here Cotton appears to have trapped himself—they are useful for exhortation, "to stir up the sons of men . . . to provoke themselves and one another to look after the Lord" (65). But, Cotton confesses, the promises, which are able to appeal outwardly only, can do nothing without the working of the Spirit inwardly. As we have seen, Puritan preachers such as Cotton demanded that their hearers exert themselves, for the preachers hoped that God would use their words as the means of grace. Here presumably Cotton hoped that his teaching concerning the promises would be matched with the coming of the Spirit, for Cotton declares that the actual union of Christ and the soul comes through the promises. Cotton's mistake was in demanding action at the same time that he denied man's ability to act.

Cotton's new awareness of the validity of High Calvinist doctrines shines through the whole volume. It is perhaps best illustrated by his passage concerning church members' children who are not effectually called by God. The Lord, preaches Cotton,

doth not only call them to church liberty and fellowship, nor only bestow upon them sundry gifts of grace and great bounties and manifold preservation from evil, but likewise He doth offer them the sure mercies of David, for so God doth distinguish the sure mercies of the covenant. Isaiah 55:3, "Incline your ear and come unto me;

hearken and your soul shall live, and I will make an everlasting covenant with you, even the sure mercies of David." Wherein you see the Lord putteth it upon such terms that if the soul come not by it, it is because he would not—not that any can come when they will, as by the power of their own will, but this the Lord will leave upon the children of Christian parents, that they shall not say that God forsook them until they have forsaken Him and that when there lay no necessity upon them but voluntarily they did despise the grace of the covenant, for do but observe the causes wherefore the Lord hath discovenanted the children of gracious parents. (222)

The grace given to those who are, through their parents, within the Covenant of Grace—"federal" grace—is not saving grace, and not such that "any can come [to God] when they will, as by the power of their own will," yet those who do not come have "forsaken Him," for "voluntarily they did despise the grace of the covenant." Passages like this are rare among Cotton's other writings; here his new strict Calvinism got the best of him and he delivered nonsense such as one cannot find in the writings of Calvin or of Augustine.

Cotton has much to say in these sermons about the inadequacy of good works as evidence of salvation, but some of his other teachings must have been intended to warn the Antinomians of the limits of orthodoxy at the same time that he was far from ready to ignore the wonderful gifts of the Spirit. He argues at length that his hearers should not look for "any revelation out of [aside from] the Word, for the Spirit comes in the mouth of the Word, and the Word in the mouth of the Spirit" (201). Yet the Spirit works "by a power above the Word" (215): "Let not men be afraid and say that we have no *revelation* but the *word;* for I do believe and dare confidently affirm that if there were no revelation but the word, there would be no spiritual grace revealed to the soul" (177–78).

A Brief Exposition . . . of Canticles

We noted that in England Cotton preached on the Song of Solomon and that his sermons were published in 1642. At an undetermined time during his American years, Cotton turned again to that Old Testament book, which must have been a favorite, since he chose a passage from it for his first American sermon in 1633. The American sermons on Canticles, not published until 1655, were entitled *A Brief Exposition With Practical Observations Upon the Whole Book of Canticles. Never before Printed.* This time Cotton sees three levels of meaning. The work describes the relationship of Christ and the church in general, that of Christ and every sincere Christian soul, and the state of the church from Solomon's time to the Last Judgment. As he had devoted his efforts to the third of these in the earlier sermons, he now spends most of his time on the first two. He is, however, less concerned with how the book should be read and more concerned with how a believer might use the book in private devotions. As Jeffrey Hammond observes, "although the great events in the progress of the collective Bride [the church] were certainly at hand, the more immediate spiritual needs of the individual Brides [church members] could not be overlooked."[7]

Cotton manages to find occasion to discuss how Christ prepares the soul for his coming, the duties of church members, the conversion of the Jews, the state of the English churches, and contemporary congregationalism. He supposes that since Canticles 8:13 says, "Thou dwellest in gardens," Christ intended each church to be a separate entity. He finds occasion to chide the New England churches: "Time was when it was thus with New English churches; but now we cannot bear wrongs, but grow contentious in suits. Now few come to us. Those that come, they corrupt us" (213).

Cotton translates the erotic poetry of the book into the story of a love affair between himself (as the person who provides the means of salvation) and his congregation. "Let him kiss me with the kisses of his mouth" is the text in which Cotton takes most delight. First he explains that "kiss of his mouth" means "not of His lip . . . not dumb salutations, but vocal and lively significations and declaratives of His love in His Word." Then he explains that the kisses are delivered not only through the prophets but through those who "interpret and apply them [the Scriptures] faithfully" (2). In other words, sermons deliver kisses. And men return God's kisses "when we receive His Word with faith, love, joy, obedience" (3). Since Christ kisses through sermons, those who love him most long for more sermons, and those whom Christ finds most beautiful are they "that seek Him in the purity of His public ordinances" (4).

As in his earlier commentary on Canticles, this sermon collection attempts to relate Canticles to church history. Some of Cotton's interpretations seem farfetched. He explains 5:15, "His legs are as pillars of marble": "These two legs (historically) were John Huss and Hierom of Prague" (156). The next step in the Reformation is described in 6:6, "My beloved is gone down into his garden"—down because it is in a lower condition than some of Christ's other gardens: "Wittenberg was a meaner place than Rome or Constantinople or Alexandria or Jerusalem or Antioch, where Christ had formerly His pleasant gardens" (164).

The most unconvincing discussion is Cotton's argument that 8:11–12 reveals Christ's relationship to his church "by a comparison of unequals or things unlike" (229). Since Solomon had a remote vineyard, Christ keeps his church under close watch. Since Solomon handed over responsibility for his vineyard to keepers, Christ keeps the church in his own hand. Solomon's keepers paid him in money; Christ keeps all the increase of his vineyard to himself.

Cotton's interest in the coming of Christ's kingdom is the most interesting subtext of the commentary. Since the development of the New England Way was a sign that the millennium was approaching, Cotton urges his hearers to wish "that Christ would hasten his last coming as swiftly and quickly . . . to take them up with himself into the highest Heavens" (257).

What was this period to be? It would be a return to the purity of what Dwight Bozeman calls "the apostolic primordium."[8] In Cotton's words, "the primitive apostolic church was . . . the most completely and abundantly fair of all that ever have been before it or shall be after it, upon the face of the earth" (92). Cotton was to have more to say about the coming of this glorious time, this return to a golden age, in his cluster of lectures on texts from Revelation, discussed later in this chapter.

Briefe Exposition . . . upon . . . Ecclesiastes

Among his posthumous works is Cotton's *Briefe Exposition with Practical Observations upon the Whole Book of Ecclesiastes*. The work is of interest because of what it reveals not only about Cotton but also about the state of mind of early New England. As early as the 1640s there was to be found in New England congregations a disturbing new complacency that led Cotton to address to his people the lessons taught by the preacher to whom all was vanity.

Cotton addresses his audience as those who left England and their worldly goods for the sake of their religion but who are now ready to leave their religion in New England for the sake of their worldly goods. But if this element leads us to expect drama and specific details about the worldliness of Cotton's parishioners, we are soon disappointed, for Cotton begins his analysis by revealing that he belongs to the tradition of the pharisaical commentators on the Scripture, not to the tradition of the prophets. In the opening lines, "Vanity of vanities, saith the preacher, vanity of vanities, all is vanity," Cotton discovers eleven ornaments of rhetoric: hyperbole, polyptoton, epizeuxis, anadiplosis, epanalepsis, anaphora, epistrophe, epanodos, numerus oratorius, climax, and paronomasia.

This kind of commentary does not strike the reader as morally edifying. Perhaps Cotton's hearers found more guidance in the interesting idea that in being idle one can manage to break five of the Ten Commandments without lifting a finger. One thus breaks the commandment against using God's name in vain, since idleness means spending one's time and talents in vain; the commandment against working on the Sabbath, since one cannot honor the Sabbath by resting unless one first has been laboring; the commandment to honor one's parents, since Proverbs 10:5 warns that a prudent son gathers in summer (presumably being a prudent son is one way of honoring one's parents); the commandment against killing, since idleness is self-murder; the commandment against adultery, since Sodom is described in Ezekiel 16:49 as being guilty of "prosperous ease" (a case of guilt by association); and the commandment against stealing, since Proverbs 19:15 says that an idle person will suffer hunger and Proverbs 10:4 says that a slack hand causes poverty.

At times Cotton manages to interpret a text in a straightforward way, as when he gleans the warning that man should view the study of the world as a proper duty but only as a means to becoming a better person. But one is much more struck by the strange and esoteric interpretations, such as the one of Ecclesiastes 12:12: "And further, by these, my son, be admonished: of many books there is no end, and much study is a weariness of the flesh." For Cotton this passage refutes the concept that we should add to the Scriptures the decrees of the popes, the Apocrypha, the Canons of the Councils, and the traditions of the church fathers as further directions for faith and living.

Cotton's concerns are not only rhetoric, ethics, and pro-Protestant scriptural interpretation but also science. He finds a confutation of Copernicus in the familiar "The sun also riseth, and the sun goeth down," and he adds: "If the earth moved swiftly, when a man throweth a stone the same way the earth moveth, he might easily overtake the stone before it fell." For Cotton the sun and the stars are alive: they must be, since they move themselves. And Aristotle was wrong to think that water seeks a lower level.

The natural order of the universe is a providential order; a man can understand God's dealings with him by observing what he is doing when some evil occurs to him, a view that seems inconsistent with Cotton's conception of the heathen moral philosophers, who are for him "vain and wicked."

The book of Ecclesiastes seems to have been for Cotton the occasion to discuss anything that interested him. We find, for example, his favorite idea that magistrates are required to put to death all blasphemers, Jewish and Christian apostates to idolatry, witches, and seducers to idolatry, for, though no man has a coercive power over another's conscience, men shall be punished for sinning against their own consciences.

Cotton finds Scripture an invaluable source of answers to questions, but one may be permitted the suspicion that the answers he found were ones he was predisposed to find. He learns that Solomon is in Heaven by noting that in Luke 13:2 Jesus says that all prophets are in Heaven, and from 2 Peter 1:19–21 and Ephesians 2:20 that the whole of Scripture was written by prophets and apostles. (The passage of Peter reads, "We have also a more sure word of prophecy; whereunto ye do well that ye take heed, as unto a light that shineth in a dark place, until the day dawn, and the daystar arise in your hearts: Knowing this first, that no prophecy of the Scripture is of any private interpretation. For the prophecy came not in old time by the will of man: but holy men of God spake as they were moved by the holy Ghost." Ephesians reads, "And [ye] are built upon the foundation of the apostles and prophets, Jesus Christ himself being the chief cornerstone.")

Cotton interprets the memorable first nine verses of Ecclesiastes 3, beginning "To everything there is a season, and a time to every purpose under the heavens," to mean that for everything there is a limited time. On the phrase *a time to dance* Cotton is explicit: "It is not said there is a lawful time but a limited time."

Ecclesiastes contains some notable statements of skepticism, but Cotton's commentary nearly overlooks them. One example may suffice. In Ecclesiastes 3:21 we read, "Who knoweth the spirit of man that goeth upward, and the spirit of the beast that goeth downward to the earth?" Cotton recognizes that the passage says that the difference between what happens to a dead man and to a dead animal "is not known or acknowledged, discerned, or considered by men generally, to wit, not by natural man at all." Yet he also reads the passage as a refutation of the concept that the spirits of the patriarchs descended to limbo: "here we see the souls of men before Christ's resurrection went upward."

The *Exposition . . . upon . . . Ecclesiastes* is not one of Cotton's more important books. Although it does reveal Cotton the scholar who is remote from the problems of ordinary men, it is not memorable for its prose or its thought. Moreover, it does not even have much of that quality which makes some of Cotton's writing interesting—a peculiar habit of thought that is fascinating in its fantasticality.

Exposition of Revelation 13

As noted earlier, in addition to his regular Sunday preaching, a noted preacher like Cotton gave weekday lectures.[9] Perhaps with the intention of maintaining the heightened piety that had been created in the early days of his ministry,[10] Cotton prepared a series of weekday prophetic, millennial sermons, published in three volumes: *An Exposition upon The Thirteenth Chapter of the Revelation; The Powring out of the Seven Vials: or, An Exposition of the Sixteenth Chapter of the Revelation, with an Application of it to our Times;* and *The Churches Resurrection,* a single sermon on Revelation 20:5–6. Dwight Bozeman emphasizes the importance of the sermons: "Probably the first founder [of the Massachusetts Bay Colony] to expound an unequivocally millennial outlook was John Cotton, who did so in a series of Thursday lectures in Boston between 1639 and 1641."[11] In these sermons Cotton reveals most clearly his understanding of his own times and of his own mission in history. As J. F. Maclear notes, "The first two works identify the final stages of terrestrial history and place the contemporary world within them; the last is Cotton's anxious welcome to the dawning glory."[12]

In England there was developing in the late 1630s and early 1640s a movement based upon the study of prophecies in the Book of Daniel concerning a Fifth Monarchy (after the monarchies of Babylon, Medo-Persia, Greece, and Rome), a time when Christ would reign on earth. Some judged that the prophecy could be brought about only by the active participation of believers and were even ready to set up the kingdom by means of the sword.[13] Though Cotton was not a "Fifth-Monarchy man," he saw the development of true churches in New England as a vital part of the historical process that would lead to the coming of Christ. Like many others engaged by millennial speculation, Cotton distinguished the anticipated glorious coming of Christ from the later coming in judgment.[14]

The prefatory epistle describes *An Exposition upon The Thirteenth Chapter of Revelation* as weekly lectures delivered at the end of 1639 and the beginning of 1640; the work was not published until 1655; the publisher was a "Fifth Monarchy" bookseller. Cotton recognizes that Revelation is an obscure book but testifies that "so much light God casts almost into the head of every man that takes this book in hand . . . that He adds some light more than hath been before brought to his hand" (4). The light that Cotton finds enables him to explain that the seven-headed beast described in Revelation 13:1 is the Roman Catholic Church, its seven heads being the seven hills and the seven kingly governments of Rome; the sea from which it arose is the corrupt doctrine, tumult, and contention from which the Roman Catholic Church arose. After more of this kind of characterization, much of it quite ingenious, Cotton concludes that the Roman church "is in the esteem of the holy Ghost a monstrous beast" (14).

Cotton then contrasts this beast with the church that he says the Lord instituted, as described in Matthew 18:15–18, the church to which one is to tell of his brother's offense as a last resort. "What!" exclaims Cotton, "The catholic visible church! When will that meet, think you? And is it ever to be expected that when they do meet, that every brother of this country and other countries must go to Rome and tell the trespasses of his brother against him, and send for those that have offended him, and thus and thus plead with them?" (15).

From this monstrous church, Cotton declares, God has delivered his followers, but also "from the remnants of the image of this beast, from all diocesan and national churches and from metropolitan and catholic visible churches that are images of this great beast" (18). But those remaining behind in England may still suffer excommunication for going to hear a sermon away from home when at home they can hear no sermons. Though Cotton finds much to observe in all of these verses of Revelation (13:3 he sees as the history of the church at the beginning of the Dark Ages), he excuses his failure to make additional comments on these lines, for, says he, "I affect brevity in mystical Scripture" (47). Instead, he focuses on contemporary Catholicism.

After various excoriations of Roman Catholicism, Cotton comes to Revelation 13:5, the latter part of which he finds "obscure as any place in the Word" (80). The passage reads: "and power was given unto him [the beast] to continue forty and two months." Cotton justifies his labor in explaining the passage: "I would not busy myself in needless speculations, but I find not any word of God a needless speculation for the church to search into and understand" (83). Cotton argues that the author of Revelation refers to 1,260 days when he writes of forty-two months; he did not use the term *days* because it was not appropriate when referring to the work of darkness, and Cotton concludes that the term *days* here equals years, for the Old Testament prophets often refer to days when they mean years. The question is, 1,260 years beginning when? Cotton believes that the period began in 395, when the pope was first called Pontifex Maximus, but it also began at the time of Constantine. Cotton therefore concludes that the ending is the year of the Pope's Bull against Elizabeth (1570), and also 1655, when Cotton foresees a great blow to Catholicism.

At times, Cotton's attitude toward Catholicism is surprisingly like some twentieth-century attitudes toward communism. After offering his interpretation of the forty-two months, Cotton suggests that this text

may teach all saints in this country or wherever not to trust the pretenses of deceitful men, especially such as are not sound in religion, and take heed also how you trust upon your own strength. (Let me put them both together for brevity's sake.) We know not how soon any of us may be tempted in this kind, what wars may be raised against this country (though we have none for the present, nor fear none), yet in time we know not what may come. What, are we better than our fathers? The Beast of

Rome still lives; his forty-two months is not yet out (though his power be much weakened), but his agents still live. (110)

Cotton attacks Roman Catholicism because it is "composed to natural sense": it appeals to the eye with its images, pictures, temples, and vestments; to the ear with its vocal and instrumental music; to the nose with its incense and perfumes; to the taste with its feasts; and to the touch by its toleration of houses of prostitution and its light penance for lewdness. He attacks Roman Catholicism also because it is attractive to natural reason. It teaches a historical faith (such as devils may have); an implicit faith (so that a man has only to believe whatever his church believes); repentance based only on contrition, confession, and satisfaction; the concept that man can keep the Law and work out his own salvation but that his salvation must remain uncertain; and a form of church government that results in unity and order.

Because Roman Catholicism has such an appeal, the Catholic Church, Cotton acknowledges, is very large; and congregationalism as a form of church government is very rare, for congregationalism is based on the ordinances of Christ, not those of men—and corrupt men prefer their own devices.

The reference to the Book of Life (Revelation 13:8) raises the question, Are only church members' names written in the book? According to Cotton, the register of members of Congregational churches and the Book of Life will be found "not exactly agreeing," for "sometimes we put in more than God doth, and sometimes less. There be [those] that belong to life whom we do not receive. Others . . . do not present themselves or we do not receive [them] through some failings in them or us, but if they belong to life, they are written in the Lamb's Book of Life" (133–34). On the other hand, no Roman Catholic's name will be found in the Book; "if they die in that religion" they "cannot go beyond a reprobate" (144), a teaching in which Cotton follows William Perkins.

The discussion of the Book of Life inspired one of Cotton's most picturesque passages:

When the Lord wrote down thy name, or mine, or any man's name, who stood by at His elbow (if I may so speak) to put Him in mind of my name or thine? He thought of us, if our names be there, and He set us down, and He delivered us to Christ Jesus by name. Whatever thy name is, He took notice of thy name. Such a man in such a place, he will live in this or that country. He is one; take notice of him; lay down a price for him. In fulness of time send a spirit into his heart. If he live in a popish country, save him from popery. If in a worldly country, save him from the world. Wherever he lives, save him from himself and bring him to my heavenly kingdom. (146)

Had Cotton written often in this vein, his sermons would have justified his contemporary reputation.

Cotton finds the phrase *the Lamb slain from the foundation of the world* (Revelation 13:8) particularly rich in meaning. If Christ was slain from the foundation of the world in terms of the efficacy and virtue of his death, then it was efficacious for such Old Testament figures as Abel, Joseph, Enoch, and Abraham. Since Enoch is said to have walked with God, he must have been one of those who benefited from Christ's death. Faith must thus have existed from Eve's time, and its object was Christ. If Christ was slain from the foundation of the world, then the world was depraved from the beginning; depravity is the universal human condition: "Folly is bound up in the heart of a child, and it is not goodness of nature or whatever else you can talk of that will root it out, nor the rod of correction, unless the blood of the Lamb be sprinkled upon it" (199). Cotton's recognition of man's sinful nature requires a limitation of all human power: "There is a strain in a man's heart that will sometime or other run out to excess, unless the Lord restrain it, but it is not good to venture it. It is necessary, therefore, that all power on earth be limited, church power or other. If there be power given to speak great things, then look for great blasphemies; look for a licentious abuse of it" (72).

The sermons on Revelation 13 thus prove to be far more interesting and important than might have been supposed. From them we learn how it was that the Massachusetts Bay colonists could conceive of their efforts— strenuous but in the context of history microscopic—as a crucial part of God's magnificent plan. Congregationalism was to them the last step in the Reformation; its limited following was an indication only that it lacked the appeal of corrupt religion.

The Powrring out of the Seven Vials

Cotton's interpretation of the prophecies of the Book of Revelation is only an incidental part of his commentary on the thirteenth chapter, but interpretation of prophecies is more important in *The Powrring out of the Seven Vials: or, An Exposition of the Sixteenth Chapter of the Revelation, with an Application of it to our Times.* These weekday lectures were published in 1645, presumably soon after they were delivered.

Cotton believed that he was living in a time when God was pouring out his wrath on everything Roman Catholic. God's angels had poured out a vial of wrath on the lowest and basest sorts of Catholics because of their "damnable ignorance, and superstition, idolatry, and hypocrisy" (13); and the instruments of God's wrath were the forces of reformation in the time of Henry VIII, Edward VI, and Mary. Then the worship and religious practices of Roman Catholicism were attacked by English and Continental theologians: William Ames, William Perkins, Whitaker, and Junius.

Attacks on Roman Catholicism, with what Cotton conceives to be its hypocrisy, led him to a warning to New Englanders, whose religious principles were so pure that they were particularly susceptible to hypocrisy. Cotton warns:

[A]ll professors [all who profess Christianity] in this country and church members . . . all that profess they came out of England for purity of ordinances, to be very circumspect, pure, and faithful, and zealous in all their whole conversation, for believe it, you will find this true and remember it while you live, if you be corrupt in New England, if you be unfaithful here, if you be wordly-minded here, false of your words and promises here, injurious in your dealings here, believe it, one of these two will unavoidably follow: either all England will judge your reformation but a delusion and an invention of your magistrates or elders, or otherwise look at you as not sincere but counterfeit. (21)

The eyes of England are on New England, Cotton still supposes.

Cotton also describes how God has been wrathful to the Catholic clergy, to the House of Austria, and to the pope's supremacy. Now the remaining three vials are to be poured out. The destruction of episcopacy, he notes, has for some time been in progress and is now being continued through the Church of Scotland, busy fighting the Bishops' Wars. All the efforts made to retain and enforce episcopacy are, Cotton observes, prophesied to occur after the pouring out of the vial against episcopacy: "They repented not of their deed." The attack on episcopacy will spread, Cotton foresees, to all Catholic countries.

The sixth vial signifies the attack on the supporters of Roman Catholicism, such as the Turks. The unclean spirits of Revelation 16:13 Cotton understands to be the cardinals, bishops, and Jesuits, who croak "not like these frogs here in America that have a several tune in each part of the year" (106).

This work ends with an extended description of the pouring out of the seventh vial and the consequent battle of Armageddon and the destruction of all iniquity. All these events will occur before long, states Cotton. What a great time to be a Massachusetts Bay Congregationalist!

The Churches Resurrection

The optimism of *The Powrring out of the Seven Vials* is extended and modified in the single sermon on Revelation 20:5–6, *The Churches Resurrection*, published in 1642, presumably about the time it was delivered. In it Cotton pictures the millennium, which he believes is about to begin. It is a time of general spiritual awakening, followed by a long period when God will neglect those whom he has not called and their descendants. The time is crucial: "if we do not strike a fast covenant with our God to be His people, if we do not now abandon whatsoever savors of death in the world, of death in lust and passion, then we and ours will be this dead-hearted frame a thousand years; we are not like to see greater encouragements for a good while than now we see" (16). The signs of the church's resurrection, which Cotton sees abroad in England and Scotland, lead him to be most hopeful; but he sees all about him at home signs of degeneration. Many in New England are ready to return to England or to go west where there are no churches. Cotton warns his hearers that they can have no part in the resurrection if they say, "We could have large elbow room enough, and meadow enough, though we had no ordinances" (26).

Cotton's millennial prophecies and hopes were shared by many in England. His prediction of a spiritual resurrection calls to mind Milton's picture of "a noble and puissant nation rousing herself like a strong man after sleep," a prophecy made in 1644, only two years after the publication of Cotton's sermon. The hopefulness of Milton's *Areopagitica* helps explain Cotton's optimism; and the parallel can be extended. Cotton's dedication of his life to the cause of further reformation permitted him to be hopeful even up to his death in 1652. In the year before his death he wrote to Oliver Cromwell in England, "I am fully satisfied that you have all this while fought the Lord's battle."[15]

The Covenant of Gods Free Grace

To some degree, Cotton's own policies, notably his tendency to tribalism, led to the failure of the New England Way. The best indication is the sermon entitled *The Covenant of Gods Free Grace*. It may well be the most mature of Cotton's sermons—it was published in 1645, probably soon after it was delivered. The late date is suggested by its theme: that God will accept a man though his household be sinful. It was about the middle of the 1640s when the Congregationalists who had come to America from England discovered that their children were not able to qualify for church membership by testifying as to their faith. The sermon, is, then, another indication of Cotton's disappointment in what was to have been God's own commonwealth.

What had happened was that the children of church members were not joining the church. Darrett Rutman provides this evidence: "Of 47 adult children (over 16 years old) found living with their parents in 1639, but 5 were members; of 32 in 1645, only 7 had joined; while of 53 in 1649, only 6 were communicants. Of children born in the commonwealth and baptized in the First Church, only one, Elizabeth Wilson, the daughter of Pastor John, sought and obtained full membership in Boston during the two decades [1630–1649] under consideration."[16]

Cotton uses as his text 2 Samuel 23:5: "Although my house be not so with God, yet He hath made with me an everlasting covenant, ordered in all things, and sure; for this is all my salvation, and all my desire, although He make it not to grow." Cotton tries to be hopeful, but at the same time he shows an awareness of an undesirable situation. God has "a secret purpose and counsel . . . to have some unbelievers in every family" (6). Still, Cotton would not have church members despair, for they can help their families to amend. (Earlier he would have argued that such amendment of life meant simply reliance on a Covenant of Works.)

The most surprising aspect of this book is its explanation of how one can join himself to the covenantal relationship. To be within the covenant meant receiving federal or common grace, Cotton had taught in his treatise on baptism. The means that Cotton suggests is a demonstration of the tribalism that Edmund Morgan has suggested was a growing weakness of American Puritanism. Cotton first suggests the study of genealogy: if any of a man's ancestors have been under the Covenant of Grace and he himself has not renounced it, he can consider that the covenant reaches to him. If not, he can claim the covenant if he has lived in a household within it. If he cannot qualify by either of these two approaches, he can still enter a household within the covenant and wait on God for a deliverance. Gone is Cotton's evangelism; God's ways are better understood now.

Presumably, those who enter the covenantal relationship by one of these methods can expect federal grace and thereby become likely candidates for saving grace. But, as Morgan observes in his discussion of the sermon, "the ministers did their best to make it difficult for an unregenerate man to enter a godly family."[17] As a consequence of the belief that grace is most likely to come to those within the covenant and to their descendants, Puritanism in time became, in Morgan's words, "hopelessly inbred," for the Puritans had "lost their concern for the gospel of Christ in a smug assurance that their children would inherit grace" (104). We have none of Cotton's last sermons, where we might see if he ever spoke with evangelistic hope to the unregenerate members of his congregation.[18]

One further sermon by Cotton, delivered in 1651, the year before his death, has recently been published. It was delivered on "A Day of Public Thanksgiving" and is intended to celebrate God's work in bringing the millennium closer through the events taking place in England, the defeat of the king by the forces of Parliament. In the sermon, Cotton is distinctly optimistic about recent events: "These are great works of God and to be taken notice of," though he admits that "it is certain the body of the nation of England is not capable of fellowship in independent churches." He refers his listeners to his sense that Presbyterian churches must be temporarily tolerated, as set forth in the preface to his book *Of the Holinesse of Church-members*.[19] In his own day, Cotton was regarded as a great preacher, as is evidenced by the care taken by his many admirers in both England and New England to print his sermons. Apparently, however, much of Cotton's appeal was in his personality. Very little of Cotton the man comes through to the reader of his sermons, though one can detect in them certain of his interests. He delighted in unraveling difficult passages in Scripture. (In 1636, Hugh Peter preached a sermon before Cotton's congregation in which he asked that Cotton be spared for a time "that he might go through the Bible and raise marginal notes upon all the knotty places of Scripture."[20]) In his own day, Cotton was regarded as a great preacher, as well as deeply interested in the place of congregationalism in Christian history.

The effectiveness of Cotton's preaching is beyond dispute. We have the testimony of John Winthrop that in 1633 "more were converted and added to that church [Cotton's] than to all the other churches in the Bay. . . . Divers profane and notorious evil persons came and confessed their sins, and were comfortably received into the bosom of the church."[21] The lectures that supplemented the Sunday sermons were preached by popular demand; they could be heard by those who belonged to other churches, who were expected to worship in those churches on Sundays.

Chapter Six

Defender of the Faith:
The Theological Writings

John Cotton's Puritanism helped him to identify himself with the Reformed tradition. Though frequently identified with Calvin and consequently often labeled Calvinist, the term *Reformed* embraces many theologians, Calvin (1509–64) being indeed foremost. Two Continental writers of special importance for England were Martin Bucer (1491–1551) and Heinrich Bullinger (1504–75). Bucer, who anticipated Calvin's views on predestination, was regius professor of divinity at Cambridge University from 1549 to 1551; as late as 1595, English theologians acknowledged their indebtedness to him. Particularly significant was Bucer's interest in the salvation process, a subject that came to dominate much of Puritan thinking. Bullinger's influence was felt especially during the reign of the Catholic Mary (1553–55), for many English exiles lived in Zurich, where he taught. The large collection of his sermons, entitled *The Decades*, was all but accepted as official doctrine by the Church of England.

The influence of Calvin himself was immense. In Elizabethan England and into the seventeenth century, Calvin's *Institutes,* his biblical commentaries, and his sermons were translated and published time and again. His teachings were accepted by bishops and by nonconforming Puritans alike. His influence was especially great because his *Institutes* offered a systematic theology to replace those of the Catholic Schoolmen and because, before the time of Richard Hooker, there was no native Protestant theologian of much importance.

Yet the influence of Calvin can easily be misunderstood. Those doctrines usually identified with his name—the concepts that Christ died only for the elect and that God's grace is irresistible—were not of much influence in the first half of Elizabeth's reign. Instead, in most Elizabethan sermons one finds what is historically thought of as Augustinianism, the doctrine that salvation comes through grace. It is this theology that dominates Alexander Nowell's semiofficial catechism, Calvin's own catechism (adopted for use at both Oxford and Cambridge), and, most significantly, the official Thirty-nine

Articles, which were thoroughly acceptable both to Puritans and to supporters of the established church.

The longest of the articles is number 17, "Of Predestination and Election." It summarizes skillfully the Reformed doctrine of the day:

Predestination to life is the everlasting purpose of God, whereby (before the foundations of the world were laid) He hath constantly decreed by His counsel secret to us, to deliver from curse and damnation those whom He hath chosen in Christ out of mankind, and to bring them by Christ to everlasting salvation, as vessels made to honor. Wherefore, they which be endued with so excellent a benefit of God, be called according to God's purpose by His Spirit working in due season: they through grace obey the calling; they be justified freely; they be made sons of God by adoption; they be made like the image of His only-begotten Son Jesus Christ; they walk religiously in good works; and at length, by God's mercy, they attain to everlasting felicity.

This article explains, as Calvin had, that the doctrine of election offers "to godly persons" the comfort of assurance of salvation.

The articles on original sin, free will, justification, and good works are consistent with Article 17. In general, the articles can be said to teach predestination, but not reprobation, and to emphasize God's grace.

These articles date from 1563, the year before Calvin's death. During the latter part of the century, a dominant figure was Calvin's successor, Theodore Beza, who spelled out the logical implications of the kind of doctrine found in Article 17. He emphasized double predestination: election to salvation and reprobation to damnation. He marks the beginning of Protestant scholasticism, and Bezaism won victory after victory over less strict varieties of Reformed thought. The consequence was that Reformed orthodoxy reached such a point of refinement that Calvin himself "would probably have made a difficulty about adopting precise and definite deliverances on some points concerning the truth of which the great Calvinistic divines of the seventeenth century had no hesitation."[1]

English theology was inevitably affected by these changes. Some theologians rebelled and adopted positions later to be called Arminian. Most fully accepted the new doctrines. The best indication of their acceptance is the Lambeth Articles of 1595, which Thomas Fuller, a knowledgeable seventeenth-century church historian, tells us contain "the general and received doctrine of England in that age."[2] The nine articles are all brief:

1. God from eternity hath predestined certain men unto life; certain men He hath reprobated.

2. The moving or efficient cause of predestination unto life is not the foresight of faith, or of perseverance, or of good works, or of anything that is in the persons predestinated, but only the good will and pleasure of God.

3. There is predetermined a certain number of the predestinate, which can neither be augmented nor diminished.

4. Those who are not predestinated shall be necessarily damned for their sins.

5. A true, living, and justifying faith, and the Spirit of God justifying is not extinguished, falleth not away; it vanished not away in the elect, either finally or totally.

6. A man truly faithful, that is, such a one who is endued with a justifying faith, is certain, with the full assurance of faith, of the remission of his sins and of his everlasting salvation by Christ.

7. Saving grace is not given, is not granted, is not communicated to all men by which they may be saved if they will.

8. No man can come unto Christ unless it shall be given unto him, and unless the Father shall draw him; and all men are not drawn by the Father, that they may come to the Son.

9. It is not in the will or power of everyone to be saved.

With this increased theological sophistication concerning the salvation process came more intense study of the psychological aspects of conversion. William Perkins, whose preaching helped prepare Cotton for conversion, was an authority not only in the new High Calvinist theology (or Bezaism) but also in the new "experimental" theology. In his *A Treatise tending unto a declaration whether a man be in the estate of damnation or in the estate of grace,* Perkins was especially concerned with the question of how far a reprobate can go down the path to salvation and how far a saint must go before he can be considered saved. Determining one's spiritual health was no longer an easy matter, as it had been for Calvin.

In his influential *A golden Chaine* (1600) Perkins combined his psychological with his theological interests. In it he explains, for example, how the reprobates are damned: "First, they have by nature ignorance and vanity of mind. After that followeth hardness of heart, whereby they become void of all sorrow for their sins. Then cometh a reprobate sense, which is when the natural light of reason and of the judgment of good and evil is extinguished.

Afterward when the heart ceaseth to sorrow, then ariseth a committing of sin with greediness. Then cometh pollution, which is the fullness of sin. Lastly, a just reward is given to all these, to wit, fearful condemnation" (167).

Treatise of Predestination

Cotton discovered early in his career that the position of Perkins was doubly difficult for him. First, Cotton found the doctrine of reprobation a difficult one to treat in a sermon. In the sixteenth-century climate of opinion, a Protestant preacher had not been expected to preach strict predestinarian doctrine, though it was more than likely that his theological position was thoroughly Calvinistic. But by Cotton's day, with the new emphasis on the decrees of God, Cotton could not avoid the issue. Second, he discovered that, in the part of Lincolnshire where he was preaching, the semi-Pelagian theology of Arminius—the position popularly called Lutheranism—was attracting many followers. Arminius conceived of the salvation process as a cooperative one, with God and the person being saved each having a role. Cotton formulated a compromise doctrine, one that might satisfy both followers of the Reformed position and those who had espoused the "Lutheran" position. In 1618, Cotton set forth his views in writing for the benefit of a neighboring minister, and this work then circulated in manuscript for many years. In 1633, William Twisse, a Perkinsian theologian, had the opportunity to read the work and to prepare a refutation, which Cotton saw before he left that year for New England. In 1646, Cotton's treatise with Twisse's reply found its way into print. Thus, *A Treatise of Mr. Cottons, Clearing certaine Doubts concerning Predestination. Together with an Examination Thereof: written by William Twisse, D.D.,* one of Cotton's earliest extant works, was finally published.

In his *Treatise* Cotton argues that God intended to create Christ before he presupposed that humanity would fall into sin. Christ was not created for us, that he might save the elect; we were created for Christ and God's glory. The decree of predestination has as its purpose the demonstration of God's justice and his grace, not his sovereignty, freedom, and dominion. Reprobation Cotton prefers to consider nonelection, and its cause is God's foreknowledge of the sins of the reprobate, or at least of some of the reprobates. The ingenuity of Cotton's scheme is worth demonstrating, for it shows the extent to which his personal feelings were apt to color his thinking. Cotton argues that God offers salvation to all the world on the conditions of obedience and repentance. Those ignorant of this offer sin nonetheless, because they sin against the law of nature in their hearts. The elect are forcibly changed by grace; the nonelect are strongly encouraged to change: "God giveth to the men of this world, I say, as opposed to the elect, such means and helps of seeking after the Lord and finding mercy from Him that they are sufficiently enabled by Him to do more than they do; that way they are deprived of those drawing and effectual means without which none can come to faith and repentance" (207). Note that Cotton does not declare that the nonelect can save themselves; their damnation is based seemingly on their failure to do what they can do. "Because of the abuse of these talents and means of grace," Cotton says, "God therefore doth deny to the men of this world such powerful and gracious helps as He vouchsafeth freely to the elect to draw them effectually to repentance and salvation" (241). The nonelect cannot obtain faith without grace; abuse of the means of grace presumably means failure to obtain faith through hearing sermons. But such a failure, such an abuse of the means, is altogether inevitable for those whom God has not chosen.

Though Cotton is said to have become persuaded that Twisse was right, he later took his old position in his treatise on baptism and in his sermons on the Covenant of Grace. Yet in his New England years he argued, with Calvin, against voluntarism. Even in this *Treatise* Cotton did not fail to identify himself with his tradition: "In the doctrine of election," he wrote, "I consent wholly with Augustine, Calvin, Beza, Martyr, Zanchy, Perkins, Paraeus, and others" (39). Cotton's departure from orthodoxy was, significantly, for the purpose of harmony among people. Cotton was primarily a preacher; his unhappiness with the dogma of reprobation was that it seemed to affect adversely his dealings with his people.[3]

A Treatise

After his arrival in the New World, Cotton soon found himself in the position of spokesman for the Puritan commonwealth that was being established there. Some of the earliest documents that he prepared as spokesman were published in 1713 as *A Treatise*. Since at this time (1634) Cotton was attempting to set down the fundamental Christian doctrines as he conceived of them, the slimness of the work belies its importance. These twelve doctrines are taken for granted in most of Cotton's other works, for, as he writes here, if one denies these doctrines, he must be considered a heretic, though one or two admonitions should precede the denunciation. The twelve are as follows:

1. God is in three persons: Father, Son, and Holy Ghost.

2. God made and governs the world; he rewards the good and punishes the evil.

3. Only God is to be worshiped.

4. The worship of God is to be performed "according to His written Word" (5).

5. Man is a sinful being and therefore a cursed one.

6. Man cannot rescue himself from this sinful state.

7. The Son became incarnate and, by perfect obedience to God, has redeemed his church.

8. Salvation is given to believers, and no man can believe except by being drawn to God.

9. "Those whom the Lord draws by his Word and Spirit to believe on Christ, them He justifies freely by His grace in Christ" (8).

10. Regeneration of the justified then follows.

11. But this regeneration is imperfect.

12. On Judgment Day men shall be judged by their works.

Prefaced to this summary is a definition of faith that makes more explicit certain of these doctrines. Cotton defines faith as a work of God "wrought by the ministry of the Word," whereby confidence in the flesh is abandoned and belief in God and his Son replace this false confidence. Cotton says nothing here about predestination, but it is implied by the seventh and eighth points, for the seventh limits the atonement to the elect, and the eighth limits the faithful to God's chosen.

This summary of Cotton's theological position indicates clearly that whereas the central events in human history are the Incarnation and the Atonement, the central event in the life of the believer is his being called to belief through the preaching of the Word. The minister's chief function is to preach, and as a preacher the minister is the most important person in a theocracy such as the Massachusetts Bay Colony.

The Case of Anne Hutchinson

Much more sophisticated are Cotton's theological works written during the Antinomian crisis of 1636–1637. These contrast sharply with the voluntarism seen in the treatise on predestination. In them Cotton argues vigorously that a person is wholly passive in the salvation process, which is God's work and not that of the person saved. Saving faith is a consequence of grace, of the union of the elect and Christ Jesus.

The Anne Hutchinson episode loomed much larger in Cotton's career than it does in his works. Six titles deal with the matter,[4] but the pamphlets *Sixteene Questions of Serious and Necessary Consequence* (1644) and *Severall Questions of Serious and Necessary Consequence* (1647) prove to be the same work, and so do the pamphlets *A Conference Mr. John Cotton held at Boston* (1646) and *Gospel Conversion* (1646). To understand these two pamphlets, one must consider the history of Cotton's dealings with Anne Hutchinson. Cotton tells the tale in *The Way of Congregational Churches Cleared* (1648), an answer to Robert Baillie's personal attack in *A Dissuasive from the Errours of our Time* (1645). The matter also comes up in the debate with Roger Williams; Cotton has some important remarks in *A Reply to Mr. Williams His Examination,* published with *The Bloudy Tenent, Washed* (1647).

In 1633–1634 the exact nature of the conversion process was becoming a much-discussed question. For a considerable period after Cotton had arrived, there was a remarkable number of conversions; sixty-three persons joined the Boston church as a result, within a six-month period. Winthrop noted, "More were converted and added [to the Boston church] than to all the other churches in the Bay."[5] In time, the period of revivals ended, and the Boston church, along with others, adopted a new practice that may have been developed first in Boston during the "revival": candidates were required to provide an account of their conversion. Many were, as a result, feeling considerable religious anxiety. Such was the situation when Hutchinson arrived.[6]

In her early years, Anne Hutchinson had lived twenty-four miles from Boston in Lincolnshire, England, in the town of Alford.[7] The daughter of a strong-minded minister, Hutchinson seems to have felt the need, from childhood, for external guidance. She did not obtain it from the man she married; indeed, she seemed to be a more domineering personality by far than her rather meek but industrious husband. In time she found the guidance she needed from John Cotton, whose sermons she heard with considerable frequency. The religious guidance that he provided was supplemented in time by the preaching of John Wheelwright, her brother-in-law, who lived within a mile of Alford. But even more comforting was the guidance that she came to feel in meditation, for here she felt God's presence. Cotton had emphasized the gratification such an experience provided.

In 1632, however, Wheelwright was removed from his position of minister, and in 1633 Cotton left for America. Unable to sustain these losses, Anne Hutchinson saw that she must go to America too. The fall of 1634 saw Anne, her husband, and her twelve children all in Boston. Here she put into use skills learned in England, and she soon was known and admired throughout the town as a helpful nurse and competent midwife. To these concerns she added an interest in the spiritual health of her followers, who soon included both men and women. It is at this point that Cotton begins his story in *The Way . . . Cleared*; the narrative is quite consistent with all of the earlier evidence concerning what happened.

Cotton explains that he had good reports of the work Hutchinson did. He was pleased that she was devoted to the spiritual as well as the physical state of the women she visited. Her special concern was to teach people not to depend on their works for their justification; she emphasized that the Covenant of Works brought with it graces that might appear to be saving but were dangerously deceptive. Since Cotton warns of the same danger in the published sermons in *A Treatise of the Covenant of Grace,* she was only following his teachings. In time she extended her efforts by reviewing Cotton's preached sermons with women of the congregation, and with some men too. These efforts seemed to Cotton very proper and helpful: "these private conferences did well to water the seeds publicly sown" (51).

Eventually she extended the conferences to include summaries of what other ministers preached. (Though Cotton does not tell us, we know that John Wilson, Cotton's colleague of the church in Boston, was much disliked by Hutchinson.) But since she did not repeat what she did not approve, she in fact became a critic of the local ministers. What she disapproved most was their way of recommending sanctification as a test of justification. Since she thought that those under a Covenant of Works were likely to detect some signs of sanctification in themselves, she rejected this test. Cotton himself had taught that sanctification was proof, but now he recognized that an emphasis on works left too much to a person's own abilities.

Cotton was not wholly happy with Hutchinson, even when she was not yet recognized as a source of heresy and discord. He warned her, he tells us, that she was prone to three errors: she trusted too much in "private meditations or revelations only" (52), she was unable to discern her sanctification as well as her justification, and she was too severe in her judgment of the spiritual condition of others. As time went on, word got to ministers outside Boston about what Hutchinson was doing. A group of them went to Cotton to report what was happening; they told him that Hutchinson and her followers were spreading heresies. But when Cotton charged the Hutchinsonians with teaching errors, they denied that they taught what was charged against them. After further counsel with the clergy, Cotton decided to attack the Hutchinsonians' teaching from his pulpit. But here, too, he got nowhere, for

Hutchinson's followers told those out of sympathy with them that "no matter . . . what you hear him say in public; we know what he said to us in private" (40).

What Hutchinson taught was judged by some to be antinomianism; that is to say, the doctrine that those who are saved by faith are not obliged to keep the Law, to recognize the Ten Commandments. It is not at all clear that such was the thrust of Cotton's beliefs, which emphasized the centrality of faith and grace; nonetheless, the events surrounding her activities, trial, excommunication, and banishment are referred to as the Antinomian Controversy.

Although Cotton does not tell us of the matter himself, his teachings were the cause of much of the trouble.[8] He did in fact differ from his colleagues in the ministry. The difference was small, but it had significant implications: it made his preaching techniques basically different from those of his colleagues, especially those of his fellow minister in the Boston church, John Wilson. Doubtless both were at heart Calvinists; doubtless both taught that people can do nothing to save themselves, but that grace must do all. The point where Cotton and Wilson differed was the question of proof. For Wilson, the proof that one had been given saving grace was his ability to do good works. For Cotton, the first evidence of grace was an awareness that the Spirit dwelt within one, the Spirit that illuminated and drew one to God. Sanctification is an effect of this indwelling of the Spirit, as is faith; but these are not at first as discernible as the sense of the Spirit's presence. Cotton's preaching put much emphasis on the gifts of the Holy Spirit to the converted, as a passage from a sermon preached in late 1638 or early 1639 and only recently published demonstrates: "The Spirit not only presents and increaseth spiritual gifts and graces but natural gifts, so as he can see angels then and God then in a vision and a light and voices then as John hears these voices."[9] As Eugenia DeLamotte observes, Cotton's "strong sense that words are not the final embodiment of revelation must have given his followers evidence that their private spiritual dramas had a legitimacy and truth greater even than that expressed in scripture itself."[10]

Cotton usually qualified his views carefully; Hutchinson started with these same doctrines but so emphasized the importance of the indwelling Spirit that she encouraged quietism, which Puritanism always regarded as a great danger. Puritans called it familism, for they identified it with a Quaker-like sect known as the Family of Love. This emphasis on the indwelling Spirit promoted individualism, judged to be dangerous because it led to heresy. It was also thought to encourage indolence, mere passive waiting. Moreover, it went against one of the underlying concepts of the colony, one growing in importance: that the social covenant would bring blessings on the people if they walked in the way of godliness.

The threat of Hutchinson's teachings was especially an attack on what I call the organicism of the Bay colony. Winthrop, in his "Model of Christian Charity," had described the personal relationships that he hoped would develop in the colony in this fashion:

> We must entertain each other in brotherly affection; we must be willing to abridge ourselves of our superfluities for the supply of others' necessities; we must uphold a familiar commerce together in all meekness, gentleness, patience, and liberality; we must delight in each other; make others' conditions our own; rejoice together, mourn together, labor and suffer together, always having before our eyes our commission and community in the work, our community as members of the same body. So shall we keep the unity of the Spirit in the bond of peace. The Lord will be our God and delight to dwell among us as His own people and will command a blessing upon us in all our ways, so that we shall see much more of His wisdom, power, goodness, and truth than formerly we have been acquainted with. We shall find that the God of Israel is among us.[11]

Hutchinson's ideas went against this much-desired unity. They even splintered into two factions the membership of the Boston church. How much out of keeping with this program and its concept of the covenant was Hutchinson's teaching may be suggested by the journal entry of a member of the Boston church. Winthrop wrote: "One Mrs. Hutchinson, a member of the church of Boston, a woman of a ready wit and bold spirit, brought over with her two dangerous errors: 1. That the person of the Holy Ghost dwells in a justified person. 2. That no sanctification can help to evidence to us our justification. From these two grew many branches, as: 1. Our union with the Holy Ghost so as a Christian remains dead to every spiritual action and hath no gifts nor graces other than such as are in hypocrites, nor any other sanctification but the Holy Ghost Himself."[12]

During the early stages of the controversy, Sir Henry Vane arrived and soon after, because of his high birth, was elected governor. He was soon an admirer of Hutchinson. His presence complicated the situation significantly.

Sixteene Questions of Serious and Necessary Consequence

Though Cotton did not know it, the ministers of the colony continued to be concerned about the evil effects of Hutchinson's teachings, especially since members of other churches were becoming her advocates. When the ministers arranged for a private conference with her, they discovered that she aligned herself with Cotton and considered the other ministers to be advocates of a decidedly different position. It was now Cotton's turn to be investigated. The questions he was asked and his answers constitute the little book *Sixteene Questions.*

The first five questions concern an expression that Hutchinson had used, "the seal of the Spirit." This phrase Cotton conceives to be the witness of the Spirit. Without this witness, a person cannot take comfort that he is saved: "The testimony of the Spirit is so clear as that it may witness immediately, though not without some work of Christ in a man, yet without respect unto the work. Nevertheless it is not so constant or permanent (at least not in all believers) but that a man after he hath received it may come in time of temptation to question his estate, though not so frequently nor so desperately as before" (6).

The next eight questions deal mainly with the relationship of good works (or sanctification) and justification. Cotton argues that sins may make one less sure that he is saved (the Spirit "will not speak wonted peace and comfort to him"), yet he will still feel assured even if he becomes degenerate. This position went against the teachings of most of Cotton's colleagues. The discernment of one's sanctification is indeed, Cotton admitted, an evidence of salvation; but no real assurance is possible "till the Spirit of God doth witness from Christ God's thoughts of peace towards him" (8). To rely on the discernment of one's sanctification is "to go on in a Covenant of Works" (9).

The other questions are of a varied nature and in no way crucial. Clearly the fundamental question is whether using sanctification as evidence of salvation is to rely on a Covenant of Works. For this question, which he reports was "exposed to greatest agitation and exception," Cotton provides an answer—one as long as the other fifteen together—to avoid "all suspicion of ambiguity and obscurity" (14). Cotton is willing for sanctification to be considered a concurrent sign of justification, but if one builds "his justifying faith upon such evidences, he shall . . . go aside to a Covenant of Works" (12). If one sees only "an evident change in himself from a profane and civil course to a sanctified conversation," he should not suppose that he has been given saving grace (9).

The elders responded to Cotton's answers that they agreed with some of his replies but "in other things we are forced to dissent."[13] Cotton's "Rejoynder," published for the first time in 1968, has been called "the most important exposition of Cotton's theology at the time of the Controversy."[14] This long, impressive, and learned document is too complex to be easily described. Cotton shows how the great reformers, such as Calvin, agreed with him. One difference between Cotton and the other ministers is clearly set forth here. Cotton finds "a broad difference between our sanctification and that of Adam, in which he neither lived by faith nor put forth any act of a heart repenting and turning to the Lord" (101–2). The issue is clearer if one consults a still-unpublished document, "Mr. Cotton's Revisall," helpfully explored by Jesper Rosenmeier, who notes that whereas the other ministers saw redemption returning those saved to the status humanity had before Adam's fall, Cotton saw in redemption the creation of Christ's image in the redeemed: "I mean by Christian sanctification the fruit of the Spirit of Christ dwelling in true believers and acting in us."[15]

The differences between Cotton and his fellow ministers on nearly all of the matters discussed were great indeed. Thomas Hooker, for example, taught that a person who has been assured of his salvation loses assurance when he sins. "When Christians grow cold in prayer and careless in holy duties," warned Hooker, "the Lord taketh away the light of His favor, and He leaves those sluggish hearts to themselves. Nay, God is forced even against His will and mind, even for the good of those Christians, to take away the comfort of His presence, so that now they begin to think they never had grace. If the Lord did not thus, they would never mend their pace, nor quicken up themselves to any holy duties."[16]

As the ministers came to realize that Cotton did differ from them in important ways, they showed great concern to reconcile their differences, the most obvious way being to try to persuade Cotton to change his views. Winthrop records for us that at a meeting of the General Court, the colony's legislature, John Wilson diagnosed the situation as extremely dangerous; he "laid the blame upon these new opinions risen up amongst us, which all the magistrates, except the governor [Henry Vane] and two others, did confirm, and all the ministers but two."[17]

The other minister was John Wheelwright, the minister to whom Anne Hutchinson had been so much attracted in England. Wheelwright had arrived in the colonies in the summer of 1636, only six months earlier. Soon he took a prominent part in the dispute. In January, Cotton reports in *The Way . . . Cleared,* Wheelwright preached at the Boston church. He taught the same doctrines that Cotton had been defending, that one should not rely on sanctification as evidence of justification. But Wheelwright went further. He recognized that a difference of opinion existed and declared war on the adversaries, who were in fact most of the ministers of the colony. "We must all of us prepare for battle," exhorted Wheelwright, "and come out against the enemies of the Lord; and if we do not strive, those under a covenant of works will prevail."[18] (In the preceding June, Cotton had preached at Salem that "Reformation is no assurance that God hath made an everlasting Covenant with us.")[19] Wheelwright's sermon was received not as a doctrinal teaching but as a battle cry. Winthrop was much distressed that Wheelwright should label as "Antichrists" those who "maintain sanctification as an evidence of justification, etc."[20] Cotton noted: "Mr. Wheelwright's sermon was apprehended to give too much encouragement to the opinionists. And himself hath since confessed that, being but new come into the country, having but little acquaintance but with his kindred [who included Anne Hutchinson] and their friends (who were many of them leavened this way) he spake some things which, if he had before discerned their familism, he would not have expressed himself as he did" (*The Way . . . Cleared,* 40).[21]

But Wheelwright knew to whom he was speaking. According to the studies of Emery Battis, 101 of the 169 members of the Boston church were supporters of Anne Hutchinson; 73 percent of the rich officeholders still supported her. Although John Winthrop was firmly opposed, another important member of the Boston church, Henry Vane, was an enthusiastic disciple; and Vane was at this time governor of the colony.

The General Court cited Wheelwright, far more vulnerable than Cotton, for sedition. Wheelwright was asked whether in his sermon he had said that some of the colony's ministers were under a Covenant of Works. His reply was that he had, if there were ministers who fit the description that he had provided. When all of the ministers except Cotton agreed that the shoe fit them, Wheelwright was found guilty. Cotton's comment on this event is most illuminating:

That I did not consent with the rest of my brethren (the elders) in drawing the inference out of Mr. Wheelwright's sermon, which they (being required) presented to the Court, I had a twofold reason for it. 1. Because I was not present with them when they searched Mr. Wheelwright's sermon and gathered that inference from it. [He had, however, heard it.] 2. Because I could not speak it of mine own knowledge. . . . They knew what themselves taught in that point better than I. The elders might testify what they knew; I could not testify what I knew not. (*The Way . . . Cleared,* 59–60)

Cotton simply wanted to avoid becoming embroiled in the dispute. But the magistrates of the General Court had been told by the Bostonians that religious opinions were not their business, and, though the magistrates rejected this view of the matter, they judged it was up to the churches to label as heresies the teachings of the Hutchinsonians. The proper instrument was the synod, as John Cotton himself taught; and in August 1637 it was to begin.

For it, the ministers prepared a collection of all the questionable opinions that had been circulating and also a collection of those of Cotton's teachings which some ministers considered erroneous.

Identifying Cotton's questionable doctrines was preliminary to the synod because the ministers wanted to present a united front. They felt that, if they could show Cotton that his doctrines were different from those of all of the rest, they could then persuade him to abandon his teachings, or at least to compromise with them. But for some reason not known, the point of disagreement was not now what it had been throughout the controversy—the role of sanctification in determining the condition of the soul—but, rather, the role of faith in the conversion process. One of the *Sixteene Questions* had indeed concerned whether God's promises are absolute or conditional; now the heart of the matter seemed to be whether faith is a qualification for justification, or, to put it another way, whether faith is a cause of salvation. On both points, Cotton was the more consistent Calvinist.

To emphasize good works as proof of one's justification and to argue that a man's faith caused his justification required man to be active, not passive. The other ministers did not abandon at this time or later the High Calvinist theology that was to be adopted by the synod of 1648. But they recognized, as Cotton did not, that in New England, as Harry S. Stout carefully explains, "all laws and customs proceeded from biblical texts, and all social arrangements were founded on voluntary covenants. There was, in their view, no conflict between Christ and the culture they had created. Thus in guiding their listeners to the ways of sanctification . . . ministers needed only to urge them to follow the Way set forth by civil and ecclesiastical 'fathers.' Civil obedience and corporate loyalty could not earn salvation but could be taken as a positive 'sign' of election." These ministers believed that Anne Hutchinson's teachings "threatened to undermine all faith in the New England Way, which depended on a bridge of trust and mutual commitment linking minister, congregation, and Word into one united organism."[22] Very probably, the cause of the dispute with Cotton was that he chose to think in abstract, theological terms; the other ministers were concerned with their social responsibilities as spokespersons for the established order.

Cotton insisted that union with Christ is complete before faith; indeed, the union is the cause of faith. In his 1636 Salem sermon he had preached, "If you come to Christ by virtue of anything which is in you, it is but a legal work" (32). He even denied what might have been a compromise: that, though union with Christ precedes faith, faith is experienced first. The presence of the Spirit itself, he declared in *The Way . . . Cleared,* is the first evidence that one has been called to salvation. In support of his teaching that faith is not the cause of salvation, Cotton quotes from Calvin that faith is "founded on the truth of a free promise in Christ" and that "this promise must be gratuitous, for a conditional promise, which throws us back upon our works, promises life only insofar as we find it existing in ourselves."[23]

Without a real agreement between Cotton and his colleagues, the synod then began. Cotton did not consider his difference from the other ministers on these points to be a matter of great concern, but at the synod he was shocked to discover that members of his congregation were ready to defend doctrines that were generally considered heretical. He warned them that to defend these doctrines was to make "all these bastardly opinions, which are justly offensive to the church" to "be fathered upon Boston" (*The Way . . . Cleared,* 47). But not all the Bostonians were willing to condemn the doctrines, and some walked out of the synod to demonstrate their displeasure at what was happening. Now Cotton saw the light. But what struck him was that his views differed not from those of the other ministers but from those of his own parishioners: "that (to my remembrance) was the first time of my discerning a real and broad difference between the judgments of our brethren (who leaned to Mistress Hutchinson) and myself." Realizing how dangerous it would be to be identified with the Hutchinsonians, Cotton quickly labeled "some of the opinions to be blasphemous; some of them heretical; many of them erroneous, and almost all of them incommodiously expressed, as intending to except those chiefly wherein I had declared my own opinion, as before" (48).

Gospel Conversion

In time, the synod denounced all of the eighty-odd doctrines that had been collected; now the ministers were to try to settle their differences with Cotton. Eventually these were reduced to three. Cotton's views on them compose the forty-eight pages of *Gospel Conversion* (1646). From the prefatory epistle, it is clear that Cotton did not intend the work for publication, but its history is otherwise obscure. It is one of Cotton's most sophisticated theological works.

Question 1 is treated briefly. Cotton contends that there are no "gracious qualifications" in the soul before faith and no gracious qualifications before union with Christ. The fullest discussion is reserved for the second question, the matter that had begun the whole controversy: whether a person may evidence his justification by his sanctification. In his defense of more than thirty pages, Cotton cites many authorities, notably John Calvin and his own old critic William Twisse. But Cotton does not budge an inch from his position that sanctification is not good evidence of justification: "I never read it," Cotton declares, "to my best remembrance in any author old or new that ever a man received his first evidence of the faith of his justification from his sanctification, unless it be one (whom I met within these two days) printed within these two years that maintaineth our first comfort of justification from sanctification. But generally all our English orthodox teachers do oppose it" (34–35).

The third question is, "Whether faith concurs as an active instrumental cause to our justification?" No, argues Cotton, "Faith may be said to be passive in our justification because it doth lay hold on Christ to fetch justification from Him till Christ have first laid hold on us and imputed His righteousness to us and declared it unto us by His Spirit in a free promise of grace. And then faith becometh active" (45).

The consequence of this extended doctrinal dispute is difficult to determine. Perry Miller says that in the end Cotton abjectly surrendered, but Emery Battis sees the outcome quite differently: "Although subjected to humiliating pressures, he was, in the last analysis, obliged to do little more than restate his original position in less equivocal terms."[24] Cotton's own comment, eleven years afterward, was that he was sorry that the dispute had ever taken place, that he was guilty for having permitted members of his church to disseminate errors without his detecting them, and "that such as endeavored the healing of these distempers did seem to me to be transported with more jealousies and heats and paroxysms of spirit than would well stand with brotherly love or the rule of the Gospel" (*The Way . . . Cleared,* 63). He does admit that in the settling of the dispute, some truth was lost. In a letter he wrote to Samuel Stone on 27 March 1638, he confessed that he had made "a disorderly expression of the order and place of faith" at the meeting following the synod.[25] This letter confirms the hazy statement in *The Way . . . Cleared* that he accepted some of the phraseology of the other ministers to settle the dispute.

Even after the synod, Cotton was not fully persuaded that Hutchinson was as wrong as the other ministers thought, perhaps because the doctrines for which she was ultimately condemned were to a large degree the product of his own teaching. His emphasis on the soul's union with Christ in justification led her to think that she could, because of this relationship, have knowledge by direct revelation. When she was tried publicly, Cotton tried to help her without identifying himself with her opinions. But she was nevertheless sentenced to be banished. When she was examined in the Boston church to see whether she should be excommunicated, Cotton saw to it that her good works as well as her errors were brought to light. Only when she defended herself by maintaining that she had arrived at her errors *after* her public trial—a statement Cotton knew to be false—did he recognize that to try to defend her was hopeless. She was then excommunicated. Clearly, Cotton had fulfilled his responsibilities to his parishioner.

The end of the story Cotton tells in both *The Way . . . Cleared* and the second part of *A Reply to Mr. Williams His Examination*. His dealings with Hutchinson, he wrote,

had bred in sundry of the country a jealousy that I was in secret a fomenter of the spirit of familism, if not leavened myself that way. Which I discerning, it wrought in me thoughts as it did in many other sincerely godly brethren of our church—not of a separation from the churches as being legal (whom we truly embraced and honored in the Lord) but of a removal to New Haven, as being better known to the pastor [John Davenport] and some others there than to such as were at that time jealous of me here. The true ground whereof was an inward loathness to be troublesome to godly minds.[26]

Winthrop and some of the other magistrates and ministers finally persuaded him to stay.

The works of Cotton that resulted from the controversy demonstrate not only Cotton's Calvinism but also his willingness to stand behind unpopular theological opinions. Those who argue that the activist preaching of the New England Puritans shows them not to have been Calvinists should note Cotton's dependence, in his carefully marshaled arguments in the Anne Hutchinson controversy, on Calvin and such later High Calvinist theologians as his critic William Twisse.

Milk for Babes

Cotton's most popular book was doubtless *Milk for Babes. Drawn Out of the Breasts of both Testaments. Chiefly, for the spirituall nourishment of Boston Babes in either England: But may be of like use for any Children* (1646). This catechism went through nine printings in the seventeenth century. *Milk for Babes* is a remarkable document. It sums up with great succinctness Cotton's main interests as a teacher in words that a child could readily understand. Cotton's catechism deals with God, man, the Ten Commandments, Jesus Christ and his office, the plan of salvation, the church, the sacraments, and the Last Judgment. Each answer is accompanied by as many as eight scriptural references. Today the work is rare indeed, and since without the references it is less than two thousand words in length, it is well worth reproducing here from the first edition.

Q. What hath God done for you?

A. God hath made me, He keepeth me, and He can save me.

Q. Who is God?

A. God is a Spirit of Himself and for Himself.

Q. How many gods be there?

A. There is but one God in three persons, the Father, the Son, and the Holy Ghost.

Q. How did God make you?

A. In my first parents holy and righteous.

Q. Are you then born holy and righteous?

A. No, my first father sinned, and I in him.

Q. Are you then born a sinner?

A. I was conceived in sin and born in iniquity.

Q. What is your birth-sin?

A. Adam's sin imputed to me and a corrupt nature dwelling in me.

Q. What is your corrupt nature?

A. My corrupt nature is empty of grace, bent unto sin, and only unto sin, and that continually.

Q. What is sin?

A. Sin is the transgression of the Law.

Q. How many commandments of the Law be there?

A. Ten.

Q. What is the First Commandment?

A. Thou shalt have no other gods but me.

Q. What is the meaning of this commandment?

A. That we would worship the only true God and no other beside Him.

Q. What is the Second Commandment?

A. Thou shalt not make to thyself any graven image, &c.

Q. What is the meaning of this commandment?

A. That we should worship the true God with true worship such as God hath ordained, not such as man hath invented.

Q. What is the Third Commandment?

A. Thou shalt not take the name of the Lord thy God in vain, &c.

Q. What is here meant by the name of God?

A. God Himself and the good things of God, whereby He is known, as a man by his name, as His attributes, worship, Word, and works.

Q. What is it not to take His name in vain?

A. To make use of God and the good things of God to His glory and our good, not vainly, not unreverently, not unprofitably.

Q. What is the Fourth Commandment?

A. Remember that thou keep holy the Sabbath day, &c.

Q. What is the meaning of this commandment?

A. That we should rest from labor and much more from play on the Lord's day, that we may draw nigh to God in holy duties.

Q. What is the Fifth Commandment?

A. Honor thy father and thy mother, that thy days may be long in the land which the Lord thy God giveth thee.

Q. Who are here meant by father and mother?

A. All our superiors, whether in family, school, church, and commonwealth.

Q. What is the honor due to them?

A. Reverence, obedience, and (when I am able) recompense.

Q. What is the Sixth Commandment?

A. Thou shalt do no murder.

Q. What is the meaning of this commandment?

A. That we should not shorten the life or health of ourselves or others but preserve both.

Q. What is the Seventh Commandment?

A. Thou shalt not commit adultery.

Q. What is the sin here forbidden?

A. To defile ourselves or others with unclean lusts.

Q. What is the duty here commanded?

A. Chastity, to possess our vessels in holiness and honor.

Q. What is the Eighth Commandment?

A. Thou shalt not steal.

Q. What is the stealth here forbidden?

A. To take away another man's goods without his leave, or to spend our own without benefit to ourselves or others.

Q. What is the duty here commanded?

A. To get our goods honestly, to keep them safely, and to spend them thriftily.

Q. What is the Ninth Commandment?

A. Thou shalt not bear false witness against thy neighbor.

Q. What is the sin here forbidden?

A. To lie falsely, to think or speak untruly of ourselves or others.

Q. What is the duty here required?

A. Truth and faithfulness.

Q. What is the Tenth Commandment?

A. Thou shalt not covet, &c.

Q. What is the coveting here forbidden?

A. Lust after the things of other men and want of contentment with our own.

Q. Whether have you kept all these commandments?

A. No, I and all men are sinners.

Q. What is the wages of sin?

A. Death and damnation.

Q. How look you then to be saved?

A. Only by Jesus Christ.

Q. Who is Jesus Christ?

A. The eternal Son of God, who for our sakes became man that He might redeem and save us.

Q. How doth Christ redeem and save us?

A. By His righteous life and bitter death and glorious resurrection to life again.

Q. How do we come to have part and fellowship with Christ in His death and resurrection?

A. By the power of His Word and Spirit, which bring us to Christ and keep us in Him.

Q. What is His Word?

A. The Holy Scriptures of the prophets and apostles, the Old and New Testament, Law and Gospel.

Q. How doth the ministry of the Law bring you towards Christ?

A. By bringing me to know my sin and the wrath of God against me for it.

Q. What are you thereby the nearer to Christ?

A. So I come to feel my cursed estate and need of a savior.

Q. How doth the ministry of the Gospel help you in this cursed estate?

A. By humbling me yet more and then raising me up out of this estate.

Q. How doth the ministry of the Gospel humble you more?

A. By revealing the grace of the Lord Jesus in dying to save sinners and yet convincing me of my sin in not believing on Him and of mine utter insufficiency to come to Him, and so I feel myself utterly lost.

Q. How then doth the ministry of the Gospel raise you up out of this lost estate to come unto Christ?

A. By teaching me the value and the virtue of the death of Christ and the riches of His grace to lost sinners, by revealing the promise of grace to such and by ministering the Spirit of grace to apply Christ and His promise of grace unto myself and to keep me in Him.

Q. How doth the Spirit of grace apply Christ and His promise of grace unto you and keep you in Him?

A. By begetting in me faith to receive Him, prayer to call upon Him, repentance to mourn after Him, and new obedience to serve Him.

Q. What is faith?

A. Faith is a grace of the Spirit whereby I deny myself and believe on Christ for righteousness and salvation.

Q. What is prayer?

A. It is a calling upon God in the name of Christ by the help of the Holy Ghost, according to the will of God.

Q. What is repentance?

A. Repentance is a grace of the Spirit whereby I loath my sins and myself for them and confess them before the Lord and mourn after Christ for the pardon of them and for grace to serve Him in newness of life.

Q. What is newness of life or new obedience?

A. Newness of life is a grace of the Spirit whereby I forsake my former lusts and vain company, and walk before the Lord in the light of His Word and in the communion of His saints.

Q. What is the communion of saints?

A. It is the fellowship of the church in the blessings of the Covenant of Grace and the seals thereof.

Q. What is the church?

A. It is a congregation of saints joined together in the bond of the Covenant to worship the Lord and to edify one another in all His holy ordinances.

Q. What is the bond of the Covenant in which the church is joined together?

A. It is the profession of that Covenant which God hath made with His faithful people to be a God unto them and to their seed.

Q. What doth the Lord bind His people to in this Covenant?

A. To give up themselves and their seed first to the Lord to be His people and then to the elders and brethren of the church to set forward the worship of God and their mutual edification.

Q. How do they give up themselves and their seed to the Lord?

A. By receiving, through faith, the Lord and His Covenant to themselves and to their seed, and accordingly walking themselves and training up their children in the ways of His Covenant.

Q. How do they give up themselves and their seed to the elders and brethren of the church?

A. By confession of their sins and profession of their faith and of their subjection to the Gospel of Christ. And so they and their seed are received into the fellowship of the church and the seals thereof.

Q. What are the seals of the Covenant now in the days of the Gospel?

A. Baptism and the Lord's Supper.

Q. What is done for you in baptism?

A. In baptism the washing with water is a sign and seal of my washing with the blood and Spirit of Christ and thereby of my ingrafting into Christ, of the pardon and cleansing of my sins, of my rising up out of affliction, and also of my resurrection from the dead at the last day.

Q. What is done for you in the Lord's Supper?

A. In the Lord's Supper the receiving of the bread broken and the wine poured out is a sign and seal of my receiving the communion of the body of Christ broken for me, and of His blood shed for me, and thereby of my growth in Christ, of the pardon and healing of my sins, of the fellowship of His Spirit, of my Strengthening and quickening in grace, and of my sitting together with Christ on His throne of glory at the Last Judgment.

Q. What is the resurrection from the dead, which was sealed up to you in baptism?

A. When Christ shall come to His Last Judgment, all that are in the graves shall rise again, both the just and the unjust.

Q. What is the Last Judgment which is sealed up to you in the Lord's Supper?

A. At the last day we shall all appear before the judgment seat of Christ to give an account of our works and to receive our reward according to them.

Q. What is the reward that shall then be given?

A. The righteous shall go into life eternal, and the wicked shall be cast into everlasting fire with the devil and his angels.

Despite this ominous ending, Cotton's *Milk for Babes* was not intended to terrify children; rather, it emphasizes the orthodox theology on the one hand and strict morality on the other. Since it is strict morality that in the popular mind characterizes Puritanism, it is worth noting that, though Cotton's sermons are always serious, he seldom deals with the demands of morality in them. The catechism is a reminder that what were considered to be the duties of a Christian were taught nonetheless, and studies of the colonial records show that moral standards were in fact extraordinarily high.

Cotton's expansion of the Ten Commandments is in keeping with his opinion that all principles of morality should be referred to the commandments. Especially characteristic is his interpretation of the Second Commandment, which limits the ways of worship to what the Bible prescribes, a view that Cotton presents again and again in his writings. Cotton follows the influential teaching of William Ames on the scope of this commandment. The restriction that Cotton finds in the Fourth Commandment, against play on the Lord's Day, not only is a reminder that his catechumen is a child but calls to mind that King James in old England had required ministers to declare from the pulpit the lawfulness of sports on the Sabbath.

Cotton's interpretation of the Fifth Commandment to demand that teachers, ministers, and magistrates be honored as well as parents seems at first to be one of the few reminders that the Bay Colony was an organic unit, with all parts considered to have an intimate interrelationship. But this idea is a Puritan commonplace, found, for example, in Perkins's *A golden Chaine.* Perhaps more enduring in New England has been the injunction to spend one's goods thriftily. Cotton's teaching on the role of the preacher in the salvation process is less helpful than one expects as a guide to his sermon practice, for Cotton in his extant sermons does not stress the wrath of God, though he does teach that man on his own is unable to come to Jesus for redemption. But for a brief statement of church polity, the catechism is most helpful.

Its influence was great, if not easy to state. Cotton Mather reports that at the turn of the century, "the children of New England are to this day most usually fed with his excellent catechism, which is entitled *Milk for Babes.*"[27] Since the law required all masters of families to catechize "their children and servants in the grounds and principles of religion," the book presumably was learned thoroughly by many a Massachusetts Bay child. In many ways, *Milk for Babes* is the most accessible and attractive brief statement of the values of the first generation of American Puritans; it deserves to be better known.

John Cotton's theological position has recently attracted a good deal of attention because it is distinctive, different from that of his New England ministerial colleagues. An authority on Calvin and Calvinism describes Cotton as "the only major figure in this study to take Calvin seriously; he read Calvin to understand what Calvin was really saying. . . . Cotton knew well where Calvin stood on most of the issues, and thought that, had Calvin been in New England in 1637, Calvin would have stood with him."[28]

Chapter Seven

Spokesman for Organicism: The Controversy with Roger Williams

John Cotton is probably best known in American intellectual history for his debate with Roger Williams over religious toleration. In this debate, Cotton expressed opinions that have been called medieval, while Williams has usually been considered the apostle of enlightened modernism. Though Williams is doubtless the more attractive figure, Cotton's position in the debate is well worth considering, for it helps us to understand Cotton's view of the Massachusetts Bay Colony.

Williams in Massachusetts

Roger Williams arrived in Boston in February 1631, seven months after John Winthrop and the other leaders of the Bay Company and more than two and a half years before Cotton reached America.[1] During his time in Massachusetts before Cotton arrived, Williams managed to make a good many enemies and very few friends. First, he refused to be made teacher of the Boston church—the post later held by Cotton—and his refusal left the church with no minister at all for a time. His reason was that the church was not separated from the corruption of the Church of England. The colonists were not ready to admit the truth of the charge, for they had never regarded themselves as Separatists, or like their Plymouth neighbors. Though Williams apparently came to New England to join his religious brethren, he refused even to become a member of the Boston church. He also criticized the established government for permitting magistrates to punish religious offenses such as Sabbath breaking. In May he accepted the position of teacher of the church at Salem, which he soon left for the separatism of Plymouth. There he served for a time as assistant minister and made himself unpopular with the authorities by preparing a treatise that branded as illegal the charter (usually referred to as the patent) by which the king had granted the land to the English. Williams was a gadfly whose admirable personal qualities were mixed with an uncomfortable iconoclasm.

Soon after John Cotton arrived in America, Williams returned to Salem. He had left Plymouth because its church was not pure enough: it did not excommunicate members who attended Church of England services during visits to England. At Salem he was again made teacher, and again he complained about the magistrates' punishing offenders against the first four of the Ten Commandments. He also taught that it was wrong for a magistrate to administer an oath to an unregenerate person. When Williams was called to give an accounting to the General Court of Massachusetts, Cotton tried unsuccessfully to persuade him of his errors. Soon the members of Williams's church at Salem began to show unhappiness with his views. When he demanded that the Salem church renounce communion with the other Bay Colony churches, the members refused, and he severed his relationship with the church. Williams demanded more of the church and less of the state than the colony's structure called for.

At a hearing given him by the court in October 1635, Williams defended his opinions, but there was no meeting of minds. He was given the opportunity to reconsider his attacks on the colony and his own relationship to it and to its churches; the matter was then to be discussed again, a month later. But Williams refused the offer. When Thomas Hooker could not persuade Williams that he was wrong, he was ordered to leave the colony within six weeks because he had defamed the magistrates and the churches and propagated opinions against the authority of the magistrates. When he continued to air his opinions, the magistrates decided to send him back to England on a ship about to depart. But before he could be taken, he fled—in the middle of the winter—to the area that was to become Rhode Island.

Cotton's role in these controversies with Williams was that of spokesman for the Massachusetts standing order, based on the principle that Massachusetts, as the New Israel, had received the promises that the Lord had made to Israel until the Israelites' apostasy: "God, who was then bound up in covenant with them [the Hebrews] to be their God, hath put us in their stead and is become our God as well as theirs, and hence we are as much bound to their laws as well as themselves."[2]

As a minister, Cotton was free to deal with Williams more tactfully than the magistrates were. Thomas Hooker played a similar part, but from later developments it appears that Williams considered Cotton the chief spokesman for the colony and, indeed, the source of his problems.

Publication of the Debate

The publication history of the debate is difficult to follow. To Williams in the Narragansett country Cotton addressed a letter, in which he tried once more to argue Williams out of his beliefs concerning the need for the New England churches to have absolute purity. This letter was later published at a time fortuitous for Williams, but he denied that he had it published. It is *A Letter of Mr. John Cottons . . . to Mr. Williams* (1643). Williams published a reply the following year, *Mr. Cottons Letter Lately Printed, Examined and Answered* (1644).

At about the time of the preparation of his reply, Williams wrote another criticism of John Cotton. This time he answered a previously unpublished work of Cotton's, itself a reply to a letter from an English prisoner who had collected arguments opposed to religious intolerance. Williams published the letter, Cotton's reply, and his own reply to Cotton as *The Bloudy Tenent of Persecution, for Cause of Conscience, Discussed* (1644). The first two of these documents, without Williams's criticism, appeared two years later as *The Controversie Concerning Liberty of Conscience in Matters of Religion* (1646).

Why did Williams publish, years after his banishment, his two attacks on Cotton? For one thing, Williams was in England, where he had access to printing presses, though even in England *The Bloudy Tenent* had to be published surreptitiously. For another, the English Independents were seeking to attract to their cause against the Presbyterians the members of the various sects that had been rapidly developing. By showing that Cotton's New England Way was one of intolerance and persecution, Williams urged the sects not to identify themselves with the Congregational Independents.

In time Cotton replied to both of Williams's attacks. In *A Reply to Mr. Williams His Examination* (1647), Cotton responded to *Mr. Cottons Letter . . . Examined*. In *The Bloudy Tenent, Washed and Made White in the Bloud of the Lambe* (also 1647), Cotton responded to *The Bloudy Tenent of Persecution*. The debate has three aspects: the purity of the New England churches, the justice of Williams's banishment, and the propriety of the Massachusetts policy of religious intolerance.

The Issues

The root of the differences between the two ministers was the relationship of church and state. Cotton conceived of the two as cooperating powers: the state protects the church from disturbance, while the church selects the leaders of the state from among its members. He did not imagine that the church could be completely pure, though church membership is limited to those who appear to have been called to salvation by God. Since ministers are not elected to serve as political leaders, a kind of separation of church and state exists.

Williams, on the other hand, advocated a more radical separation; he judged that genuine purity is possible in the church. His views are much less clear than Cotton's on the nature of the church, for—as he declared in *Queries of the Highest Consideration* (1644)—he was a Seeker dissatisfied with all known concepts of the church. (The Seekers believed that they must seek further light from God before they could determine which was the true church.) With this belief that truth was not known but was to be known, Williams was all but forced to become an advocate of tolerance.

Cotton insisted that the New England churches are Reformed churches and that their members have repented the practices they had prior to their establishing pure religion in America. What is needed, Cotton urged, is for church members to hate what separates them from Christ, not to denounce those Christians who have not yet rejected all impure practices. Thus "we conceive the Lord hath guided us to walk with an even foot between two extremes; so that we neither defile ourselves with the remnant of pollutions in other churches, nor do we for the remnant of pollutions renounce the churches themselves, nor the holy ordinances of God amongst them, which ourselves have found powerful to our salvation. This moderation, so far as we have kept it in preaching or printing, we see no cause to repent of, but if you show us cause why we should repent of it, we shall desire to repent that we repented no sooner."[3]

Cotton's God is far more generous and forgiving than Williams's: "The grace of Christ is not given either to his church or to any Christian upon the perfection of our repentance nor upon our repentance of our greatest sins, in the greatest measure. But if the heart be truly humbled for any known sin, as sin, though the sin unknown be less heinous than others known, yet God accepteth his own work and putteth away all sin in the acknowledgment of one."[4] He later added in the same work, "I do believe the repentance of the ministers (for sins known and secret) and the faith of the godly party, is more able to sanctify the corrupt and unclean sort to their communion than the corruption of the unclean sort is able to corrupt the minister and worship and church-estate of all" (223–24).

Cotton charged that Williams's policies were too demanding; he had stopped "the bread of life from feeding hungry souls." (That is, Williams would have prevented those who had evidence of salvation from receiving the Lord's Supper.) Williams replied: "I would not, and the Lord Jesus would not, that one drop or one crumb or grain should be unlawfully, disorderly, or prodigally disposed of."[5] Others accused the New England churches of demanding too much of their members; Roger Williams alone found them demanding too little.

Their disagreement about church membership eventually centered on their varied interpretations of the parable of the tares in Matthew 13. Cotton's view of the church was that church membership inevitably included hypocrites as well as saints. He understood the tares in the parable to be these hypocrites, who cannot be removed without plucking out some saints as well; for saints are like flowers "who sometimes lose their . . . sweetness for a season."[6] Cotton feared that the truth of the parable was demonstrated at the time of the Antinomian crisis, when excommunication might have eliminated both tares and wheat, hypocrites and saints.

Williams believed that it is possible to detect the hypocrites and that to permit them to remain within the church "is contrary to all order, piety, and safety in the church of the Lord Jesus."[7] The radical purity of the church thus differs from the fundamental corruption of the world as whole. The world of Williams is a wilderness; the church (insofar as Williams describes it at all) is a bright spot of purity. God so protects it that it is needless for people to offer it protection from the world around it: God is able to save his elect in any circumstance.

In Cotton's world, individual persons are the potential means through which God acts. The pouring out of God's wrath, predicted in the Book of Revelation, is to come through the efforts of godly people, persecutors of corruption, even such as the New England Congregationalists. Cotton believed that it is lawful to punish those in a Christian commonwealth who attack religious truth because the state should protect the church from disturbances and because on fundamental points of religious doctrine and worship, the Bible is so clear that once one's error is explained to him by citing Scripture, he "cannot but be convinced of the dangerous error of his way."[8] After such an explanation, one cannot plead that he has a right to attack orthodoxy (Cotton's variety) for the sake of his conscience; indeed, to attack orthodoxy after admonition is to defy one's own conscience, and so one is liable to punishment.

There are three religious sins that Cotton would have the state punish: blasphemy, idolatry, and the seduction of others to one's errors. The first two are the ones on which, Cotton says, the Bible is perfectly clear. He would punish those who spread heresy because he put little faith in human reason. He did not praise a fugitive and cloistered virtue: he saw the world as inevitably a dangerous place where risks are unavoidable. He sought to preserve the

peace of a community that had unity, as he believed his did. Though Cotton
would vigorously reject modern pluralism, he was seeking a place in a plural-
istic society for a unified community, founded on a voluntary covenant. He
saw in Massachusetts the establishment of the modern equivalent of ancient
Israel, and he wanted to protect the community in accord with the injunction
of Deuteronomy 13:9–10: "Thou shalt surely kill him . . . because he hath
sought to thrust thee away from the Lord thy God."

Cotton considered the magistrates of Massachusetts the equivalent of the
kings of Israel. Like the Old Testament prophets, Cotton taught that, since
God is just, he will visit an apostate land with punishment; to protect their
people—their bodies as well as their souls—the magistrates must not permit
apostasy. The rulers are responsible to God for both body and soul. Cotton
considered that Christ "never abolished a national civil state nor the judicial
laws of Moses." Massachusetts, which has agreed to submit to the laws of
God, has "as much truth and reality of holiness as Israel had. And therefore,
what holy care of religion lay upon the kings of Israel in the Old Testament,
the same lyeth now upon Christian kings in the New Testament."[9] As a Puritan, Cotton looked to the Bible for commandment and precedent, and for
him the Old Testament provided magistrates (who are "New Testament
kings") with perfect models.

Williams, too, looked to the Bible, but unlike Cotton he saw a radical separation between the Old and the New Testaments. As Edmund Morgan has
explained, Williams, like other Protestants, judged that "Israel had been a
nation specially favored by God and that in Israel God had combined state
and church in a single holy institution. Williams believed that with the coming of Christ, God had dissolved the combination, that to accomplish the distinction was in fact one of His purposes in sending Christ into the world."[10]
That Williams supposed he could persuade Cotton and the New Englanders
to accept his notion of the distinction between the Old Testament and the
New is difficult to imagine. Cotton and the other Congregationalists taught
as fundamental doctrine that the same covenant of faith was offered in both
testaments; they looked to the Old Testament and to the example of
Abraham as the authority for their idea of the church covenant.

Cotton's position on the relationship of church and state and his opposition to religious tolerance were closely identified with almost every aspect of
his thought. He could scarcely have taken a different position in the debate
with Williams. But Cotton would not have appeared quite so unmodern had
Williams not seen fit to blame Cotton for his being thrust out into the New
England wilderness in midwinter. Williams went so far as to argue that had
he died "in that sorrowful winter's flight," Cotton would have been guilty of

his death, for Cotton "without mercy and human compassion" caused him to "be exposed to the mercy of a howling wilderness in frost and snow."[11] This charge Cotton answered, but he has not persuaded historians, who should know that he was innocent of the charge. Cotton appears to have had truth on his side:

The truth is [declares Cotton] the sentence of his banishment out of the patent was pronounced against him in the Court before winter, and respite was given him to tarry certain weeks (six or more) to prepare for his journey. In the meantime, some of his friends went to the place appointed by himself beforehand to make provision of housing and other necessaries for him against his coming; otherwise he might have chosen to have gone southward to his acquaintance at Plymouth, or eastward to Pascatoque or Aganimticut. And then the wilderness had been as no wilderness (at least, no howling wilderness) where men sit down under warm and dry roofs, sheltered from the annoyance of frost and snow and other winter hardships.[12]

At the time of Williams's exile, as Edmund Morgan observes, the Bay colony had not "been split apart or lured into such an irresponsible pursuit of individual holiness as Williams advocated. The great majority of the population, even the great majority of the Salem church, kept their eyes on the goal that Winthrop had set them . . . a common goal which all must seek together."[13] But by 1646 the goal was being neglected by many. Disillusionment over their great experiment, dissatisfaction with the colony's government, attacks from the right and the left—all of these meant that the unity of the colony was rapidly disappearing. This disappearance must have been evident to John Cotton, but in *The Bloudy Tenent, Washed* he kept his eyes on his ideal, not on reality. Williams's desire to deny the state a holy purpose and to limit it to worldly, temporal functions struck at the very heart of Cotton's concept of a united purpose that binds all aspects of life to one another. Williams won the debate, though his *Bloudy Tenent* was burned in London by the public hangman: the prestige of the New England Way had suffered from the exposé. Williams had the last word in the debate in *The Bloody Tenent Yet More Bloody, By Mr. Cottons endeavor to wash it White in the Blood of the Lambe* (1652). The trend of history, too, was on Williams's side, for when the Holy Commonwealth of Massachusetts Bay became a royal province in 1692, the process of secularization was completed. Today Williams is viewed as the prophet of the order that was to be.

Chapter Eight

Moses and Aaron Kiss Each Other: The Political Writings

Though John Winthrop is usually recognized as the chief spokesman for New England theocracy, it was John Cotton who was called on at a crucial time to describe and defend the system of political government that had been established. Cotton did not himself have a hand in the ordering of the Massachusetts Bay colony political structure, just as he had not arranged the original ordering of the ecclesiastical structure. He was indeed influential in polities of both church and state, but perhaps these activities were less important than his services as a kind of forerunner of the modern public relations expert.

Because he was thoroughly sympathetic with the ideals of the Bay colony, Cotton assumed an important role almost as soon as he arrived. In 1634, Winthrop consulted him when Roger Williams attacked the colonists' right to the lands they were inhabiting. Cotton was called on again in 1636 to help decide how strict the discipline of the colony should be. Indeed, Winthrop, who was governor during many of the early years, consulted Cotton frequently on many matters—as well he might, since he was a member of Cotton's church.

In addition, Cotton frequently found occasion in his sermons to deal with political matters. Thus he explained that the magistrates, who disagreed with the town representatives in a matter before the General Court, had a veto power and could prevent the adoption of a measure though they were outvoted.[1] Cotton was not alone in his close relationship as minister to the political powers. Norton, Cotton's biographer, tells us that "it was an usual thing . . . for the magistrates to consult with the ministers in hard cases, especially in matters of the Lord; yet so as, notwithstanding occasional conjunction, religious care was had of avoiding confusion of counsels. Moses and Aaron rejoiced and kissed one another in the Mount of God. . . . [H]ow useful he [Cotton] was to England, to New England, to magistrates, to ministers, to people, in public and in private, by preaching, counsel, and resolving difficult questions, all know that knew him."[2] Perry Miller puts Cotton's role more simply; he was "the mouthpiece of the ruling oligarchy."[3]

Answer to Lord Say

The letter to Lord Say and Seal—discussed in the chapter on congregationalism because of the letter's treatment of the political covenant—was written in answer to a letter that Lord Say, Lord Brooke, and "other persons of quality" had written in 1636 to Henry Vane. Cotton also wrote answers to ten demands that the lords had sent to Vane. Cotton had first sought out "such leading men amongst us as I thought meet to consult withal,"[4] but the letter itself was his responsibility.

The lords had proposed that they, along with others of their social rank, should constitute the equivalent of the House of Lords in the new colony, with the lords having veto power. These gentlemen would become the hereditary aristocracy of the colony. The other class to have political power, the freeholders, was to be limited to large landowners who "have contributed some fit proportion to the public charge of the country either by their disbursements or labors" (1:412).

The Americans would have none of it, though they could see that their present system of political power could in part be interpreted as consistent with what the lords wanted. But Cotton's reply is thoroughly diplomatic:

As for accepting them ["these noble personages and worthy gentlemen"] and their heirs into the number of gentlemen of the country, the custom of this country is, and readily would be, to receive and acknowledge not only all such eminent persons as themselves and the gentlemen they speak of, but others of meaner estate, so be it of some eminency, to be for them and their heirs gentlemen of the country. Only thus standeth our case. Though we receive them with honor and allow them preeminence and accommodations according to their condition, yet we do not, ordinarily, call them forth to the power of election or administration of magistracy, until they be received as members into some of our churches, a privilege which we doubt not religious gentlemen will willingly desire (as David did in Psalm xxvii. 4) and Christian churches will as readily impart to such desirable persons. Hereditary honors both nature and Scripture doth acknowledge (Ecclesiastes xix. 17), but hereditary authority and power standeth only by the civil laws of some commonwealths, and yet, even amongst them, the authority and power of the father is nowhere communicated, together with his honors, unto all his posterity. Where God blesseth any branch of any noble or generous family, with a spirit and gifts fit for government, it would be a taking of God's name in vain to put such a talent under a bushel, and a sin against the honor of magistracy to neglect such in our public elections. But if God should not delight to furnish some of their posterity with gifts fit for magistracy, we should expose them rather to reproach and prejudice, and the commonwealth with them, than exalt them to honor, if we should call them forth, when God doth not, to public authority. (412)

These were brave words in 1636. They suggest a dedication to an ideal at a time when the colony was in real need of financial assistance. The understanding that Cotton shows of the nature of the venture was surely one of the reasons for his power and influence.

An Abstract, or The Lawes of New England

On 6 May 1635, according to John Winthrop, "the deputies having conceived great danger to our state in regard that our magistrates, for want of positive laws in many cases, might proceed according to their discretions, it was agreed that some men should be appointed to frame a body of grounds of law, in resemblance to a Magna Carta, which, being allowed by some of the ministers and the General Court, should be received for fundamental laws."[5] Those appointed to prepare the Massachusetts Magna Carta were the governor, John Haynes; two former governors, John Winthrop and Thomas Dudley; and a future governor, Richard Bellingham. Nothing was accomplished. A year later, another committee was appointed, this time with Governor Henry Vane, Winthrop, Dudley, Haynes, and three ministers: Thomas Shepard, Hugh Peter, and John Cotton.

As a member of this committee, Cotton presented to the General Court in October 1636 what Winthrop called "a model of Moses his judicials, compiled in an exact method" (*Journal,* 1:196). The code circulated for five years but finally was not adopted, because it was not what was needed. A recent commentator suggests that Cotton's proposal "failed of acceptance, not because of excessive biblicism, but because it fell short of meeting the demands of the popular party bent upon abridging the magistracy's discretionary privileges." Cotton had proved "far more adept in discovering scriptural grounds for the magistrates' than for the freemen's prerogatives."[6] Instead, what Cotton prepared was in the main a compilation of the laws already established, supplemented by many proposals consistent with these laws. The work was published twice, in 1641 and in 1655, first as *An Abstract, or The Lawes of New England as they are now established* (the edition I cite) and later as *An Abstract of Laws and Government.* Though not adopted, it had considerable influence, as we shall see. What was adopted, *The Book of the General Lawes and Libertyes Concerning the Inhabitants of the Massachusetts* (1640), includes a preface that borrowed from Cotton. Cotton had proposed, in a letter to Winthrop, the following paragraph, a most revealing one:

That distinction which is put between the Laws of God and the laws of men becomes a snare to many as it is misapplied in the ordering of their obedience to civil authority, for when the authority is of God and that in way of an ordinance (Romans 13.1) and when the administration of it is according to deductions and rules gathered from the Word of God and the clear light of nature in civil nations, surely there is no human law that tendeth to common good (according to those principles) but the same is mediately a law of God and that in way of an ordinance which all are to submit to and that for conscience' sake.[7]

Sometime between his presentation of the laws and the court's rejection of them, Cotton defended his proposal; and a manuscript copy in Cotton's hand of his defense is extant. Entitled "How Far Moses Judicialls Bind Massachusetts," it was published by Worthington C. Ford in 1903.[8] In it Cotton distinguishes two types of Old Testament law, temporary and perpetual. The latter he considers binding on Massachusetts, and he offers nine reasons. Some of them are as follows: "because God, who was then bound up in covenant with them [the Hebrews] to be their God, hath put us in their stead and is become our God as well as theirs, and hence we are as much bound to their laws as well as themselves"; "if God hath given us no other for the governing of the commonwealth, then we either may be lawless and have what laws we please or else be bound to these, but God hath given us no other nor are we lawless, for we are under the Law to God and to Christ"; adoption of God's laws "will be our wisdom in the sight of the nations (Deuteronomy iv. 6) so as they shall say, this is a wise people"; and "if the Jews be now still under the bond of them and so to observe them when they are an established commonwealth, then we are bound to observe them . . . because there is no other revelation that there shall be other laws" (281). Added later is a thoroughly Puritan reason for following biblical law: "The more any law smells of man, the more unprofitable" (284).

In an interesting passage, Cotton describes the relationship of the Old Testament to Christianity. As reconstructed, the passage reads:

If it was part of the misery of the Gentiles to be aliens from the commonwealth of Israel (Ephesians ii. 12), then 'tis a part of the happiness of Christian nations that they are subject to the laws of that commonwealth of Israel; and to be strangers from the commonwealth of Israel is not to be a church because that is to be strangers from the promise, that is, from the covenant of the church and so from the civil covenant. Christ is king of church and commonwealth. So far as it [the church] varies from the commonwealth of Israel, so far is Christ from being king of the church. So far as the commonwealth varies from the laws of the church, so far is Christ from being king of the commonwealth. Christ is head of all principalities and powers for the church, and He will subordinate all kingdoms one day to the church. (284)

Here is the basis for the organicism of the colony.

Cotton's *Abstract* is divided into ten chapters. The first, concerning the magistrates, as a whole follows Massachusetts policy, but it provides lifetime tenure for the assistants "because these great affairs of the state cannot be attended nor administered if they be after changed" (2). To support his position, Cotton cites 1 Kings 12:6: "And King Rehoboam consulted with the old men, that stood before Solomon his father while he yet lived, and said, How do ye advise that I may answer this people?" Here Cotton remained consistent with what he had preached at the General Court in 1634, that "a magistrate ought not to be turned into the condition of a private man without just cause, and to be publicly convict, no more than the magistrates may not turn a private man out of his freehold, etc., without like public trial, etc."[9] The court had answered Cotton by choosing several new magistrates and by turning out the old ones.

Cotton says surprisingly little in *An Abstract* about the relationship of the magistrates to the church, merely that the governor has power. But this power is great indeed, as later chapters in the work make clear. More is said about the kind of person to be chosen magistrate: a free burgess (Cotton's equivalent of freeman) "out of the ablest men and most approved amongst them," and "out of the rank of noblemen or gentlemen among them, the best that God shall send into the country, if they be qualified with gifts fit for government, either eminent above others, or not inferior to others" (1). It is not surprising that Cotton should make this recommendation, for in 1634 he had lectured the inhabitants of Boston for their failure to elect Winthrop "and other of the chief men" to a committee on land distribution.[10]

Chapter 2, "Of the Free Burgesses and Free Inhabitants," defines the power of the burgesses as electors and the power of the General Court elected by the burgesses. In this chapter Cotton explains more of his view of the relation of church and state. The General Court is "to assist the governors and counselors in the maintenance of the purity and unity of religion, and accordingly to set forward and uphold all such good causes as shall be thought fit for that end by the advice with consent of the churches, and to repress the contrary" (3–4).

Although it is often maintained that Cotton's code is purely Old Testament legalism, he does not attempt to support any of the articles of this chapter by reference to Scripture. The same can be said for chapter 3, most of chapter 4, and most of chapter 5. English common law and the established practices of the colony are nearly as important as the Bible as foundations for *An Abstract*.

Chapter 3, "Of the Protection and Provision of the Country," deals with taxes, the military, and fishing. In it Cotton proposes a law to encourage commercial fishing by providing people "to plant and to reap" for the fishermen, mariners, and shipbuilders for the next seven years (4). Though nothing so generous appears to have been done, a law was passed in 1639 that remitted the taxes for seven years on all fishing supplies and materials.[11]

Religion is a concern even in chapter 4, "Of the Right of Inheritance." Here we also find that no one is permitted to dwell more than a mile from a church meetinghouse, for "all civil affairs are to be administered and ordered so as may best conduce to the upholding and setting forward of the worship of God in church fellowship" (6). (A law of 1635 actually required that "no dwelling house shall be built above half a mile from the meeting house.")[12] In dividing the lands of a town, Cotton would have two considerations determine the amount of land to be awarded: the size of the family (plus the number of animals owned) and the character of the prospective landowner. "Eminent respect in this case may be given to men of eminent honorable accommodations in regard of their great disbursements to public charges," he wrote (6). This proposal was carried out when lands owned by Boston at Muddy River were divided. Cotton and other members of the gentry were given substantial lands—Cotton was given 250 acres, while the less prosperous citizens were granted much smaller pieces.[13]

Much of chapter 4 is concerned with arrangements to prevent the loss of taxes should land be sold to someone other than an inhabitant of the town wherein the land lay. But one provision in this chapter is curious and difficult to explain. Instead of following English common law that permitted a man to will his estate as he saw fit, Cotton provides that the eldest son is to have a double portion. He cites in support Deuteronomy 21:17. Cotton's plan of inheritance was in fact adopted by the General Court for cases in which the parents die intestate.[14]

Chapter 5, "Of Commerce," again may indicate Cotton's influence on Massachusetts policies, or it may indicate merely that Cotton accepted what appeared to be the only solution to a difficult situation. From its early years, Massachusetts had fixed prices and profits, but variation in supply and demand made regulation difficult. Cotton urged the establishment of township committees to handle the problem, a solution that in time was partially adopted by the General Court, which assigned wage-level problems to the towns.[15] In 1639, because Robert Keayne was found guilty of making too large a profit on commodities, Cotton preached from the pulpit on false and sound principles of buying and selling.[16] The chapter in *An Abstract* discusses other matters of business ethics, such as borrowing; but it does not offer a truly adequate program for a business community.

The chapter "Of Trespasses" is fuller than might be expected, presumably because Cotton found many Hebrew laws on the subject in Exodus and Leviticus. Similarly full is the list of crimes deserving capital punishment. Nineteen crimes are cited in chapter 7, including seventeen supported by biblical citations: blasphemy; idolatry; witchcraft; consulting with witches; heresy with attempt to seduce others; worshiping God in a molten or graven image; Sabbath breaking; rebellion, sedition, and insurrection; rebelliousness on the part of children; murder; adultery; incest; sodomy and buggery; intercourse with a woman during her monthly period; "whoredom of a maiden in her father's house"; man stealing; and bearing false witness. Only three nonbiblical crimes are to be punished by death: willful perjury, treason, and reviling the governor or his counselors.

The list sounds impressively severe. In fact, English law of the time was much more severe. It mandated death for stealing more than a shilling, for housebreaking, and for many other crimes. Most of the crimes on Cotton's list were cause for capital punishment in England. Although in England rebellious children were not subject to the death sentence, as they were in Massachusetts, and although English adulterers were liable only to heavy fines, unnatural sex acts, heresy, and witchcraft were all capital offenses.[17] The only peculiarly Puritan crime in Cotton's list is Sabbath breaking, and the Puritans of England shared Cotton's concern to keep the day holy. *The . . . Lawes and Libertyes . . . of Massachusetts* followed Cotton in prescribing death for adultery.[18]

Lesser crimes were to be punished less severely than in England, according to chapter 8. Cotton names only seven lesser crimes: profanity, drunkenness, rape, fornication, maiming or wounding, theft, and slander. All of these were also punishable by English law. Cotton proposes as punishments—depending on the crime—fines, whipping, branding, or boring through the tongue. A rapist, for example, is to be punished with "fine or penalty to the father of the maid. 2. With marriage of the maid defiled, if she and her father consent. 3. With corporal punishment of stripes for his wrong, as a real slander" (12).

Chapter 9, concerning trials and execution of sentences, reveals clearly that Cotton is familiar with and favorably disposed toward English common law. He provides for an impartial jury in criminal and civil cases, and he forbids the imprisonment of any person unless he has been convicted or is suspected of having committed a crime named specifically in the code.

The final chapter, "Of Causes Criminal Between Our People and Foreign Nations," is perhaps the most interesting and probably the most original. Cotton briefly explains the justification for war: when the people of another nation do "any important wrong to any of ours" and "right and justice be denied and it will not stand with the honor of God and safety of our nation that the wrong be passed over, then war is to be undertaken and denounced" (14). For such a war, men are to be spared from the army if they are betrothed but not married, or recently married, or "have newly built or planted and not received the fruits of their labors," or if they are "fainthearted men."

Cotton devotes three sections to the spoils of war. He is particularly interested in sparing fruit trees and women, "especially such as have not lain by men." He gives the church its share of the spoils, a larger one if all of the soldiers survive and return.

The *Abstract* is an interesting and important work, and not merely a curiosity. Isabel Calder argues that it "deserves recognition as the earliest compilation of New England legislation."[19] She notes that Cotton's code was adopted in 1639 as a permanent constitution for the New Haven colony, and that it was also used by the company that settled at Southampton, Long Island, in 1640. A more recent commentator, George L. Haskins, finds it remarkable that Cotton, "who had no legal training and who was not an officer of the colony, should have had as complete a grasp as he did of the fundamentals of its government, of the laws already in existence, and of the need in certain directions for guarantees of due process and civil rights."[20]

A Discourse about Civil Government

Closely related to *An Abstract* is *A Discourse about Civil Government in a New Plantation Whose Design is Religion* (Cambridge, Mass., 1663).[21] The *Discourse* is a letter apparently to the Reverend John Davenport, a founder of the New Haven colony and a house guest of Cotton's in 1637. Davenport seems to have been sympathetic to Cotton's legal code in every respect but one. He was not sure that Cotton (and Massachusetts) was correct to restrict to church members the right to vote and to hold office. Cotton's letter of explanation and defense is valuable for the light it sheds on his view of the relationship of church and state. It is a significant document, one overlooked by most scholars.

Cotton distinguishes the role and function of church and state as follows: "Man by nature being a reasonable and sociable creature, capable of civil order, is or may be the subject of civil power and state, but man by grace called out of the world to fellowship with Jesus Christ and with His people is the only subject of church power" (6). Cotton defines the state as a "human order appointed by God to men for civil fellowship of human things" (6). Church and state are thus parallel institutions but with separate purposes.

The best form of government for a Christian commonwealth is, according to Cotton, a "theocraty," the form of government that exists when "all the free burgesses be such as are in fellowship of the church or churches which are or may be gathered according to Christ," and when "those free burgesses have the only power of choosing from among themselves civil magistrates" (14).

If the magistrates are all church members, then they will rule by God's laws. They have power over their old failings and are endowed with the power of the Holy Spirit. If all magistrates are church members, they can work together in peace and harmony and also consult with the ministers of God "in all hard cases and in matters of religion" (15). A state like this is the form of government prescribed by the Old Testament example of Israel, Cotton points out, and also the type of government that gives Christ what Saint Paul says is due to him.

Though Christ is above both church and state, there is no confusion of the two in Cotton's plan. The corruption of the papacy developed, he says, when the civil power delegated authority to ecclesiastical officers. But as members of the church, civil officers are spiritually subject to ecclesiastical officers. One provides outward honor, justice, and civil peace; the other, the means of grace, pardon of sin, and peace with God.

Cotton's description of the relationship of church and state indicates his great concern with the problem. It should be emphasized that he was addressing people who were planning a colony "whose design is religion." Unlike some critics of the early American Puritans, we would do well to note what their motives were before we judge them to have been hypocrites.

Cotton's political writings reveal more clearly than those of any other New England writer the organic nature of the Massachusetts Bay Colony in its early years. Church and state, laws and economic forces—all were interrelated. To call Cotton the high priest of Puritan theocracy is perhaps a judgment and not a description; Cotton would have preferred to think of himself as one who understood that in the Old Testament, Moses and Aaron each had a role to play.

Chapter Nine
Tamer of Impious Sentiments: The Verses

New England Puritans wrote and read a good deal more poetry than used to be supposed, but little of the poetry produced, except for Anne Bradstreet's and Edward Taylor's, has much literary value. Like Taylor, most of the lesser Puritan poets tried to fuse wit and sentiment. For example, John Fiske, whose poetry was rediscovered by Harold Jantz, wrote an elegy on the death of John Cotton in the form of variations on an anagram of the deceased preacher's name: "O, Honie Knott." Though the poem seems more ingenious than powerful, Fiske's "But now, oh and alas to thee to call / In vain 'tis" presumably was meant to sound quite heartfelt.[1]

Kenneth Murdock has suggested that the inadequacies of American Puritan poetry can be explained partly by a consideration of the poet's audience. A poet wrote "to be of service to the rank and file of his readers."[2] In a closed community such as the Massachusetts Bay Colony tended to be, the preacher frequently felt obliged to speak words of consolation to his flock or to that of a dead colleague. Thus Fiske, pastor at Salem, wrote consolatory verses on the deaths of the Reverends Nathaniel Rogers, Thomas Hooker, Samuel Sharpe (ruling elder of Fiske's own church), and John Wilson.

Wilson, Cotton's colleague in the ministry of the church at Boston, was a poet of some note in his lifetime, more because he was a pious preacher who chose to write verse than because he was accomplished in the art of poetry. John Cotton too was interested in poetry, as his book *Singing of Psalmes* shows. He may have made some of the translations of the Psalms as they appear in the *Bay Psalm Book,* but he also recognized that "every good minister hath not a gift of spiritual poetry."[3]

Cotton first wrote five extant poems, according to Harold Jantz,[4] and Donald Come has located a fragment of another, to which he refers in his unpublished Princeton dissertation on Cotton.[5] The fragment, probably written in the 1610s, is interesting for its content rather than for its art. Apparently written before Cotton became a nonconformist, it seems to identify him as a moral Puritan, not an opponent of ceremonies, if indeed he considered himself a Puritan at all. The verse is as follows:

> Of Puritans two sorts I find,
> The moral and the ceremonial kind:
> The ceremonial, God's great name to hallow,
> Will strain at motes, as well as beams not swallow.
> His tender conscience makes his fleshly heart
> At smallest pricks and scruples back to start.

The earliest of the five complete poems is a consolatory verse written after Cotton had decided to give up Lincolnshire for Massachusetts Bay. Poetry was for Cotton, as for other Puritans, a means of taming one's emotions by forcing them into the pattern demanded by art. The fact that he needed this kind of discipline at the time of his self-exile suggests that his leaving Lincolnshire was a wrenching experience for him. The poem is not so bad as to suggest that this kind of writing was utterly unfamiliar to Cotton. The third and fourth of the eight stanzas read:

> When I think of the sweet and gracious company
> That at BOSTON once I had,
> And of the long peace of a fruitful ministry,
> For twenty years enjoy'd:
>
> The joy that I found in all that happiness
> Doth still so much refresh me
> That the grief to be cast out into a wilderness
> Doth not so much distress me.

The second poem, also consolatory, was written for those who bewailed the loss of Thomas Hooker in 1647. Prefixed to Hooker's *Survey of the Summe of Church Discipline,* the poem "On my Reverend and dear Brother Mr. Thomas Hooker" is in many ways Cotton's best. Following the fashion of the day, it combines wit with piety. The thesis of the poem is that in Hooker was found the equivalent of what Saint Augustine had wished to see: "Rome in her flower" (Hooker offered more, for the beauty of Zion shone in his rule and doctrine); "Christ Jesus in the flesh" (Hooker's preaching provided what was better, the Spirit of Christ); and "Paul i' the pulpit" (Hooker inherited a double portion of Paul's spirit). The poem ends with this coda:

> Now, blessed Hooker, thou art set on high,
> Above the thankless world and cloudy sky:
> Do thou of all thy labor reap the crown,
> Whilst we here reap the seed which thou hast sown.

The third poem Cotton Mather located on a spare leaf of John Cotton's almanac. In three parts, the poem—in Mather's words—"most exemplarily expressed what was required" when Rowland and Sarah, Cotton's youngest son and eldest daughter, died of smallpox during the fall of 1649. The occasion was apparently too much for the father, for the poem is probably Cotton's weakest. It reads, in part:

> On th' twentieth of th' eleventh died she,
> And on the twenty-ninth day died he.
> Both in their lives were lovely and united,
> And in their deaths they were not much divided.

The fact that Cotton felt obliged to be witty is surely one reason for the failure of the poem.

More successful because the wit seems more natural is the poem on Samuel Stone, Hooker's colleague in the ministry of the Hartford church. The poem, a eulogy written for Stone when he was still alive to enjoy it, plays with the minister's name by identifying him with stones having religious significance. Stone is "for solid firmness fit to rear / A part in Zion's wall"; he is—most playfully—"Like Samuel's stone, erst Ebenezer hight, / To tell the Lord hath help'd us with His might."

Finally, Cotton wrote a five-stanza autobiography in verse entitled "A thankful Acknowledgment of God's Providence." It suggests that the disappointments that marked his last years did not altogether sour him.

> In mother's womb Thy fingers did me make,
> And from the womb Thou didst me safely take:
> From breast Thou hast nurs'd me life throughout,
> That I may say I never wanted ought.
>
> In all my meals my table Thou hast spread,
> In all my lodgings Thou hast made my bed:
> Thou hast me clad with changes of array,
> And chang'd my house for better far away.
>
> In youthful wanderings Thou didst stay my slide,
> In all my journeys Thou hast been my guide:
> Thou hast me sav'd from many an unknown danger.
> And show'd me favor, even where I was a stranger.
>
> In both my callings Thou hast heard my voice,
> In both my matches Thou hast made my choice:

Thou gav'st me sons and daughters, them to peer,
And giv'st me hope thou'lt learn them Thee to fear.

Oft have I seen Thee look with mercy's face,
And through Thy Christ have felt Thy saving grace,
This is the Heav'n on earth, if any be:
For this, and all, my soul doth worship Thee.

Cotton's poetry is the least of his accomplishments, but for this last poem we can be grateful, for it suggests that the gentleness and the serenity that so often come through in his sermons were based on an experiential religion, about which Cotton has almost nothing to say, at least directly, in his other writings.

Chapter Ten

John Cotton's Significance and Contribution to American Literature

It is a commonplace that Puritanism has had a profound influence, both on American culture in general and on American literature more specifically. American literature, it has been observed, differs from English literature to a substantial extent because of the Puritan influence,[1] recognized clearly in the writings of Nathaniel Hawthorne but recognizable too in the work of Benjamin Franklin and Ralph Waldo Emerson, to name two important writers that come to mind. But it would be difficult to identify this "Puritan influence" as specifically that of John Cotton.

John Cotton was recognized in his day, in both England and America, as a most admirable and attractive figure. In both Bostons he was deeply admired by the members of his church. What most impressed his contemporaries was his piety, the result of his strong sense that God had both called him to salvation and revealed himself to Cotton in a most remarkable way. Cotton's contemporaries, such as John Winthrop and Thomas Shepard, have left records of their spiritual struggles; one senses that Cotton experienced no such struggles.

Cotton's special gift was his belief that in his lifetime, through the events taking place in Britain *and* in New England, God was ushering in a time when such purity as that known heretofore only in the churches of the apostles would again be the experience of humanity. Though he had been unable at the time of the Antinomian Controversy to persuade his ministerial colleagues that they too should hold out to their congregations the glorious experience of God's grace, Cotton seems not to have been discouraged. Recently Andrew Delbanco, who has explored what he calls "the Puritan ordeal," has identified Cotton as a heroic figure who was on the right side of the disputes among the Massachusetts ministers. Delbanco finds that Cotton's celebration of God's grace and his conviction that sin is deprivation and not stain provided hope "for the realized Christian community as the destiny of man."[2]

Cotton slowly developed a vision that in his time the Christian church would be resurrected, would return to the purity of its earliest years. Cotton attempted to provide, in Dwight Bozeman's words, "some account of that end-time perfection itself as a state to be enjoyed during the several centuries before the Second Coming and the end of history."[3] What was happening in Massachusetts, where both church and state were devoted to God's pure principles, was prefatory to this great time.

The sense of mission that John Cotton felt throughout his American career—and during a good part of his years in England—was based on his sense of how Christ could reign. From the days of his ministry in Lincolnshire, Cotton's thinking was dominated by his dream of purity, of the covenanted community. But always mixed with this idealism was a tendency to be cautious, to be conservative. This quality is indicated by Cotton's waiting until three years after the Massachusetts Bay Colony had been established before making his move to join it. But it must be emphasized that Cotton made a remarkable sacrifice in choosing to cross the water, as anyone who has seen St. Botolph's Church in Lincolnshire and, by comparison, sketches of the primitive meetinghouse that served the church Cotton came to minister to in Massachusetts must recognize. This mixture of conservatism and idealism characterized New England culture until at least the time of Ralph Waldo Emerson, though in the eighteenth century conservatism seemed for a time triumphant.

Cotton was able to take a major role in the attempt to create a Holy Commonwealth in Massachusetts because of his substantial abilities, already widely recognized before he came to America, and because he was minister of the colony's most important and influential church, that of Boston. Since he was frequently called on to speak for the Massachusetts standing order, his writings are regularly consulted by those who wish to know the principles underlying the work of the colony's leaders. Yet he had distinct personal limitations. He was not a creative or original thinker but rather a scholar inspired by other people's ideas—John Calvin's, Richard Sibbes's, and William Ames's. He did have, however, a strong sense of the moment, what Larzer Ziff calls an "eschatological tone," "a sense of the American experience as one of changes hastening along to one millennium or another."[4] His qualities do not make Cotton a wholly attractive figure—most people prefer the originality and apparent liberalism of a Roger Williams to Cotton's caution. Many who have looked at Cotton's role in the Antinomian Controversy judge that he failed his follower Anne Hutchinson because he was not willing to become a martyr for his dedication to the power of the Holy Spirit. But, as Daniel Boorstin observes, had the Puritans had other qualities, "they might have merited praise as precursors of modern liberalism, but they might never have helped found a nation."[5]

No single work of Cotton's demonstrates all these qualities, and no one work stands out as his masterpiece. Some of Cotton's best writings can, of course, be identified. The letter to Lord Say and Seal, the first three sermons in *Gods Mercie Mixed with his justice,* early pages from *The Powrring out of the Seven Vials, Milk for Babes,* autobiographical passages in *The Way . . . Cleared,* and parts of *The Bloudy Tenent, Washed*—these are among Cotton's best. All are distinguished by their intellectuality, their clarity, and their authority. John Cotton's style is commendably classical in its restraint; yet one misses the thunder and fire such as one gets from Thomas Hooker. Moreover, it must be admitted that some of Cotton's interpretations of the Bible and his efforts at argument are so time-bound as to seem almost ridiculous to the modern reader, even one who tries to see Cotton in the context of his own time and place.

One comes back to an appreciation of Cotton's sense of mission, to the understanding that his works give of the religious nature of the undertaking in Massachusetts. Beside the heroic efforts of the Plymouth Pilgrims, the settlers of Massachusetts Bay may appear to have been dominated by economic motives. Cotton's works reveal that economic factors were indeed recognized as having importance in the venture, but it was part of the breadth of the Puritan design that church and state, law and government, manners and morals, and business and labor, should all find a place in the New England Way.

The "Way" involved the perpetual balancing off of the democratic tendencies and the autocratic ones, the Separatist tendency to assume a superior purity and the natural tendency to assume that whatever is being done is right. (It is characteristic of Cotton to insist that magistrates are to have extensive powers but still limited powers: they should be given "as much power as God in His Word gives to men," not more.)[6] Shut off from the larger world of Europe, Cotton did well to prevent American values from becoming identified with extremism and with fanaticism. On the other hand, one should recognize that Cotton was far more daring than those who followed him. Kenneth Murdock writes with respect of the earlier New England Puritans as nonconformists (in the popular sense of the word), and he quotes with approval Ralph Waldo Emerson's opinion that the essence of Boston is its principle of rebellion, started before "pioneer Puritanism hardened down into an organized and intolerant ecclesiastical and credal system."[7]

John Cotton as the most respected and the most prolific writer of his generation in America can hardly be said to have had an important influence on American literature. Nor have literary scholars found much to admire in Cotton's writings, though a recent commentator points to those writings as "a major record of the forces that shaped New England."[8] Cotton has fared better among the historians, who find his writings to be among the best sources for an understanding of Puritan New England. One cannot disregard Cotton's contemporary reputation. Edward Johnson celebrated him in *History of New England,* better known by its running head, "Wonder-working Providence of Sions Saviour, in New England" (1654):

> When Christ intends his glorious kingdom shall
>   Exalted be on earth, he earth doth take,
> Even sinful man to make his worthies all;
>   Then praise I man, no Christ this man doth make,
> Sage, sober, grave, and learned Cotton thou;
>   Mighty in Scripture, without book repeat it,
> Anatomy the sense, and show man how
>   Great mysteries in sentence short are seated.
> God's word with's word comparing oft unfold;
>   The secret truths John's Revelation hath
> By thee been open'd, as nere was of old;
>   Shows clear and near 'gainst Rome's whore is God's wrath.
> The churches of Christ, rejoice and sing,
>   John Cotton hath God's mind, I dare believe,
> Since he from God's Word doth his witness bring;
>   Saints' cries are heard they shall no longer grieve.
> That Song of Songs, 'twixt Christ and's church thou hast
>   Twice taught to all, and sweetly showed the way.

But Johnson's celebratory poem is too long to quote entirely.

Cotton's devotion to scholarship, his willingness to take risks, his idealism and his conservatism—these are in the great American tradition. His coolness makes his prose less lively than Thomas Hooker's and Thomas Shepard's, but the greater variety of his works gives them real importance. Whoever would understand the rationale of the Massachusetts Bay Colony cannot ignore the writings of John Cotton.

Notes and References

Chapter One

1. *Magnalia Christi Americana* (London, 1702), 3:25–26.
2. Ziff, *The Career of John Cotton* (Princeton, N.J.: Princeton University Press, 1962), viii, 159. Much of the biographical information in this chapter is derived from this excellent biography.
3. On education at Cambridge, see William J. Costello, *The Scholastic Curriculum at Early Seventeeth-Century Cambridge* (Cambridge, Mass.: Harvard University Press, 1958), and Harris F. Fletcher, *The Intellectual Development of John Milton,* vol. 2 (Urbana: University of Illinois Press, 1961).
4. Mather, *Magnalia,* 3:274.
5. Norton, *Abel being Dead yet speaketh; or, The Life & Death of . . . Mr. John Cotton* (London, 1658), 10.
6. Pishey Thompson, *The History and Antiquities of Boston* (London: Longman, 1856), 180.
7. Quoted in Mark Spurrell, "*The Puritan Town of Boston*" (Boston, Lincolnshire: Richard Kay, 1972), 9.
8. John F. Bailey, *Transcriptions of the Corporation of Boston* (Boston, Lincolnshire: History of Boston Project, 1981), 2:127–28, 189.
9. *Magnalia,* 3:25–26.
10. Norton, *Cotton,* 20.
11. "The Records of the First Church in Boston, 1630–1868," in *Publications of the Colonial Society of Massachusetts,* ed. Richard D. Pearce, 39 (1961):1,10.

Chapter Two

1. The history of English Puritanism is set forth and illustrated in Everett Emerson, *English Puritanism from John Hooper to John Milton* (Durham, N.C.: Duke University Press, 1968).
2. See Charles L. Cohen, *God's Caress: The Psychology of Puritan Religious Conversion* (New York: Oxford University Press, 1986), 5–14, and chapter 6 of the present study.
3. Theodore Dwight Bozeman, *To Live Ancient Lives: The Primitivist Dimension in Puritanism* (Chapel Hill: University of North Carolina Press, 1988), 9–12; Andrew Delbanco, *The Puritan Ordeal* (Cambridge, Mass.: Harvard University Press, 1989), 59–80; Jack P. Greene, *Pursuits of Happiness: The Social Development of Early Modern British Colonies and the Formation of American Culture* (Chapel Hill: University of North Carolina Press, 1988), 21–22.

4. See Winton U. Solberg, *Redeem the Time: The Puritan Sabbath in Early America* (Cambridge, Mass.: Harvard University Press, 1977), 27–80.

5. Published by Winton U. Solberg in "John Cotton's Treatise on the Duration of the Lord's Day," *Sibley's Heir, Publications of the Colonial Society of Massachusetts* 59 (1982):505–22.

6. Ann Kibbey argues that only the first treatise in *Some Treasure* is by Cotton. See *The Interpretation of Material Shapes in Puritanism: A Study of Rhetoric, Prejudice, and Violence* (Cambridge: Cambridge University Press, 1986), 155–59.

7. Cotton's notions of baptism are considered in the context of sacramental history in E. Brooks Holifield, *The Covenant Sealed: The Development of Sacramental Theology in Old and New England* (New Haven, Conn.: Yale University Press, 1974).

8. Quoted by Samuel Whiting in his "Concerning the Life of the Famous Mr. Cotton," in *Chronicles of the First Planters of the Colony of Massachusetts Bay,* ed. Alexander Young (Boston: Little and Brown, 1846), 427.

9. The matter is well discussed by Larzer Ziff, *The Career of John Cotton* (Princeton, N.J.: Princeton University Press, 1962), 57–70.

10. *Letters from New England: The Massachusetts Bay Colony, 1629–1638,* ed. Everett Emerson (Amherst: University of Massachusetts Press, 1976), 127–30.

11. *Journal* (New York: Scribner, 1908), 1:279.

12. One of the reasons for Cotton's rejection of written prayers is that their use implies a form of church government other than Congregational. It is unlawful "to worship God in a form of words devised by the officers of one congregation and prescribed and imposed upon others" (13).

13. Horton Davies, *The Worship of the English Puritans* (Westminster [London]: Dacre, 1948), 162.

14. Introduction, *The Whole Booke of Psalmes* (Cambridge, Mass., 1640), sig. [**⁴].

15. Introduction, *Booke of Psalmes,* sig.[*⁴], verso.

Chapter Three

1. *The Rise of Puritanism* (New York: Columbia University Press, 1938), 15.

2. Hooker, *The Application of Redemption: The Ninth and Tenth Books* (London, 1656), 11.

3. See James F. Maclear, "'The Heart of New England Rent': The Mystical Element in Early Puritan History," *Mississippi Valley Historical Review* 42 (1956): 626–27, 635–39.

4. Sibbes, *Works* (Edinburgh: J. Nichol, 1862–64), 1:53.

5. Ibid., 7:99.

6. Ibid., 1:425.

7. Smith, *Works* (Edinburgh: J. Nichol, 1866–67), 1:304–5.

8. Ibid., 1:23–24.

9. Adams, *Works* (London, 1629), 433.

10. Prefatory epistle to Cotton's *An Exposition upon the Thirteenth Chapter of the Revelation* (London, 1655).

11. *A Practical Commentary upon . . . John* (London, 1656), 47, 76, 41.

12. Norton, *Abel being Dead yet Speaketh; or, The Life & Death of . . . Mr. John Cotton* (London, 1658), 17–18.

13. Perkins, *Arte of Prophesying,* in Perkins, *Works* (London, 1612–1613), 2:673.

14. *Arte of Prophesying,* 2:651. Another Puritan, John Udall, contributed the notion of providing reasons for the doctrines. See Everett Emerson, "John Udall and the Puritan Sermon," *Quarterly Journal of Speech* 44 (1958):282–84. See also Eugene E. White, *Puritan Rhetoric: The Issue of Emotion in Religion* (Carbondale: Southern Illinois University Press, 1972), 19–23.

15. William Chappell, *The Preacher* (London, 1656), 26.

16. *Of the Holinesse of Church Members* (London, 1650), 68–69. The discussion that follows of Cotton's use of figurative language is much indebted to Eugenia DeLamotte, "John Cotton and the Rhetoric of Grace," *Early American Literature* 21 (1986):49–74.

17. DeLamotte, "Cotton and Rhetoric," 52.

18. Habegger, "Preparing the Soul for Christ: The Contrasting Sermon Forms of John Cotton and Thomas Hooker," *American Literature* 41 (1969):345.

19. Toulouse, *The Art of Prophesying: New England Sermons and the Shaping of Belief* (Athens: University of Georgia Press, 1987), 41.

20. Ibid., 33.

21. Ibid., 32.

22. Habegger, "Preparing the Soul," 359.

23. The discussion of Cotton's commentary here is informed by Jeffrey A. Hammond, "The Bride in Redemptive Time: John Cotton and the Canticles Controversy," *New England Quarterly* 56 (1983):78–102, and Mason I. Lowance, *The Language of Canaan: Metaphor and Symbol in New England from the Puritans to the Transcendentalists* (Cambridge, Mass.: Harvard University Press, 1980).

24. Theodore Dwight Bozeman, *To Live Ancient Lives: The Primitivist Dimension in Puritanism* (Chapel Hill: University of North Carolina Press, 1988), 229–30 (n. 85).

25. Thomas M. Davis, "The Traditions of Puritan Typology," in *Typology and Early American Literature,* ed. Sacvan Bercovitch (Amherst: University of Massachusetts Press, 1972), 11–45; Lowance, *Language of Canaan,* 13–27.

26. Ames, *The Marrow of Sacred Divinity,* trans. John Eusden (Boston: Pilgrim Press, 1968), 205; originally published in Latin in 1612.

27. Typological interpretations were to appear in many of Cotton's writings, notably in his debate with Roger Williams.

28. *Application of Redemption,* 28.

29. Baynes, *A Counterbane* (London, 1618), 19.

30. For an exploration of the sermons in this collection and their relationship to Cotton's association with Preston, see Jesper Rosenmeier, "'Clearing the Medium': A Reevaluation of the Puritan Plain Style in Light of John Cotton's *A Practicall Commentary Upon the First Epistle Generall of John*," *William and Mary Quarterly*, 3d ser., 37 (1980):577–91.

31. Cotton Mather, *Magnalia Christi Americana* (London, 1702), 2:25–26.

32. Weber, *The Protestant Ethic and the Spirit of Capitalism* (London: Allen and Unwin, 1930), 232.

33. Heppe, *Reformed Dogmatics* (London: Allen and Unwin, 1950), 521.

34. Hooker, *The Soules Implantation* (London, 1637), 108.

35. Calvin, *The Deity of Christ and Other Sermons* (Grand Rapids, Mich.: Eerdman, 1950), 151–52.

36. This difference is a major theme in Andrew Delbanco, *The Puritan Ordeal* (Cambridge, Mass.: Harvard University Press, 1989).

37. I cite the reprint in Old South Leaflets (Boston: Directors of the Old South Work, 1894–1896), Vol. 3, no. 53.

38. Sacvan Bercovitch, *The American Jeremiad* (Madison: University of Wisconsin Press, 1978), 8–9; Jesper Rosenmeier, "VERITAS: The Sealing of the Promise," *Harvard Library Bulletin* 16 (1968):33–35.

39. See Richard W. Cogley, "John Eliot and the Origins of the American Indian," *Early American Literature* 21 (1986–87):211–13, and the writings of Cotton cited there.

Chapter Four

1. See Cotton's *The Way of the Congregational Churches Cleared* (London, 1648), 11, and Robert S. Paul, ed., *An Apologeticall Narration* (Philadelphia: United Church Press, 1963), 65(n.18).

2. David Cressy, *Coming Over: Migration and Communication between England and New England in the Seventeenth Century* (Cambridge: Cambridge University Press, 1987), passim.

3. Winthrop, "A Model of Christian Charity," *Winthrop Papers* (Boston: Massachusetts Historical Society, 1929–1947), 2:293.

4. Cotton himself provides evidence of this undertaking in *The Way Cleared* (London, 1648), 20. An excellent discussion of the historical development of this notion of a church covenant is found in John S. Coolidge, *The Pauline Renaissance in England: Puritanism and the Bible* (Oxford: Clarendon Press, 1970).

5. Williston Walker, ed., *The Creeds and Platforms of Congregationalism* (New York: Scribner, 1893), chap. 6.

6. "John Cotton's Letter to Samuel Skelton," ed. David D. Hall, *William and Mary Quarterly*, 3d ser., 22 (1965):481, 483.

7. See Edmund S. Morgan, *Visible Saints: The History of a Puritan Idea* (New York: New York University Press, 1963), 86.

8. John Winthrop, *Journal* (New York: Scribner, 1908), 1:107.

9. "The Records of the First Church in Boston, 1630–1868," ed. Richard D. Pearce, *Publications of the Colonial Society of Massachusetts* 39 (1961):1:10.

10. Darrett Rutman, *Winthrop's Boston: A Portrait of a Puritan Town, 1630–1649* (Chapel Hill: University of North Carolina Press, 1965), 32–34, 39, 57, 72, 98; *Boston Church Records* 1:xxviii.

11. Stearns, *The Strenuous Puritan: Hugh Peter, 1598–1660* (Urbana: University of Illinois Press, 1954), 174.

12. Haller, *Liberty and Reformation in the Puritan Revolution* (New York: Columbia University Press, 1955), 155.

13. I use the text in *John Cotton on the Churches of New England,* ed. Larzer Ziff (Cambridge, Mass.: Harvard University Press, 1968).

14. Cotton to Skelton, 482.

15. See Larzer Ziff, "The Salem Puritans in the 'Free Aire of a New World,'" *Huntington Library Quarterly* 20 (1957):373–84.

16. Cotton to Lord Say and Seal, in *Letters from New England,* ed. Everett Emerson (Amherst: University of Massachusetts Press, 1976), 191, 192.

17. Morgan, *The Puritan Dilemma* (Boston: Little, Brown, 1958), 90–96.

18. *A Coppy of a Letter,* as found in Emerson, ed., *Letters from New England,* 198.

19. Letter to Winthrop in *Winthrop Papers,* 3:399.

20. Miller, *Orthodoxy in Massachusetts* (Cambridge, Mass.: Harvard University Press, 1933), 100.

21. *Records of the Governor and Company of Massachusetts Bay* (Boston: William White, 1853–1855), 1:168.

22. Ziff, "The Social Bond of the Church Covenant," *American Quarterly* 10 (1958):454–62.

23. Stoddard, *The Doctrine of Instituted Churches* (London, 1700), 7.

24. Edwards, *Antapologia* (London, 1644), 31–32, 40.

25. See *The Book of the Lawes and Libertyes Concerning the Inhabitants of Massachusetts,* ed. Thomas G. Barnes (San Marino, Calif.: Huntington Library, 1975), 24.

26. Ames, *Marrow,* trans. John Eusden (Boston: Pilgrim Press, 1968), 208, 180, 210.

27. Giles Firmin recorded that Nathaniel Ward said to Hooker, "You make as good Christians before men are in Christ as ever they be after"—Firmin, *The Real Christian* (London, 1670), 19.

28. Cotton's epistle in John Norton, *The Answer,* trans. Douglas Horton (Cambridge, Mass.: Harvard University Press, 1958), 11.

29. Walker, ed., *Creeds, 169–70.*

30. *Ibid., 185.*

31. *I cite the text in Walker, Creeds, 195–96.*

32. Quoted in Ziff, "Social Bond," 461.

Chapter Five

1. Cotton Mather, *Magnalia Christi Americana* (London, 1702), 3:31.
2. Andrew Delbanco, *The Puritan Ordeal* (Cambridge, Mass.: Harvard University Press, 1989), 13.
3. The precise differences, as Charles L. Cohen observes, are "Cotton's denying that sanctification offers primary evidence of justification, that assurance may be grounded in conditional promises, and that regeneration is a progressive renewal of the original Adamic perfection"—*God's Caress: The Psychology of Puritan Religious Experience* (New York: Oxford University Press, 1986), 263.
4. Hooker, *The Soules Preparation* (London, 1632), 157.
5. Ibid., 155.
6. Ziff, *The Career of John Cotton* (Princeton, N.J.: Princeton University Press, 1962), 113.
7. Hammond, "The Bride in Redemptive Time: John Cotton and the Canticles Controversy," *New England Quarterly* 56 (1983):100.
8. Theodore Dwight Bozeman, *To Live Ancient Lives: The Primitivist Dimension in Puritanism* (Chapel Hill: University of North Carolina Press, 1988), 258.
9. On the character of the weekday sermon, see Harry S. Stout, *The New England Soul: Preaching and Religious Culture in Colonial New England* (New York: Oxford University Press, 1986), 48, 325 (n. 19).
10. So suggests Philip F. Gura in *A Glimpse of Sion's Glory: Puritan Radicalism in New England, 1620–1660* (Middletown, Conn.: Wesleyan University Press, 1984), 129.
11. Bozeman, *Primitivist Dimension, 229.*
12. Maclear, "New England and the Fifth Monarchy: The Quest for the Millennium in Early American Puritanism," *William and Mary Quarterly,* 3d ser., 32 (1975):232.
13. Bryan Ball, *A Great Expectation: Eschatological Thought in English Protestantism to 1660* (Leiden, The Netherlands: E. J. Brill, 1975), 181–85. For further background, see Katharine R. Firth, *The Apocalyptic Tradition in Reformation Britain, 1530–1645* (Oxford: Oxford University Press, 1979), which however, does not discuss Cotton.
14. Bozeman, *Primitivist Dimension, 232–33.*
15. Cotton to Cromwell, 28 July 1651, in Thomas Hutchinson, ed., *A Collection of Original Papers relative to the History of the Colony of Massachusetts* (Boston, 1769), 234.
16. Rutman, *Winthrop's Boston: A Portrait of a Puritan Town* (Chapel Hill: University of North Carolina Press, 1965), 148.
17. Morgan, *The Puritan Family: Religion and Domestic Relations in Seventeenth-Century New England,* new edition, revised (New York: Harper and Row, 1966), 161–86.

18. On the confusion between the external (church) covenant and the internal covenant (of grace), see E. Brooks Holifield, *The Covenant Sealed: The Development of Puritan Sacramental Theology in Old and New England, 1570–1720* (New Haven, Conn.: Yale University Press, 1974), 155–59.

19. "Sermon upon a Day of Publique thanksgiving," in Francis J. Bremer, "In Defense of Regicide: John Cotton on the Execution of Charles I," *William and Mary Quarterly*, 3d ser., 37 (1980):122–23.

20. Winthrop, *Journal*, 1:179.

21. Ibid.

Chapter Six

1. William Cunningham, *The Reformers and the Theology of the Reformation* (Edinburgh: T. and T. Clark, 1866), 412. For a brief recent discussion of the subject, see R. T. Kendall, "The Puritan Modification of Calvin's Theology," in *John Calvin: His Influence in the Western World,* ed. W. Stanford Reid (Grand Rapids, Mich.: Zondervan, 1982).

2. Fuller, *Church History of Britain* (Oxford: At the University Press, 1845), 5:227.

3. The Twisse episode is discussed in R. T. Kendall, *Calvin and English Calvinism to 1649* (Oxford: Oxford University Press, 1979), 112–17.

4. Another work by Cotton, "Mr. Cottons Rejoynder," is included in *The Antinomian Controversy, 1636–1638,* ed. David D. Hall (Middletown, Conn. Wesleyan University Press, 1968); the collection also includes *Sixteene Questions,* with manuscript augmentations.

5. Winthrop, *Journal* (New York: Scribner, 1908), 1:116.

6. See Edmund S. Morgan, *Visible Saints: The History of a Puritan Idea* (New York: New York University Press, 1963), 97–100; Hall, *Antinomian Controversy,* 13–16.

7. This account is derived largely from Emery Battis, *Saints and Sectaries: Anne Hutchinson and the Antinomian Controversy in the Massachusetts Bay Colony* (Chapel Hill: University of North Carolina Press, 1962), in addition to Cotton's own story. Two studies that provide a valuable sense of the context of the Antinomian Controversy are Stephen Foster, "New England and the Challenge of Heresy, 1630 to 1660: The Puritan Crisis in Transatlantic Perspective," *William and Mary Quarterly*, 3d ser., 38 (1981):624–60, and Philip F. Gura, *"A Glimpse of Sion's Glory": Puritan Radicalism in New England, 1620–1660* (Middletown, Conn.: Wesleyan University Press, 1984), especially 239–75.

8. A full discussion of Cotton's theological position is set forth by William K. B. Stoever, *"A Faire and Easie Way to Heaven": Covenant Theology and Antinomianism in Early Massachusetts* (Middletown, Conn.: Wesleyan University Press, 1978); see especially 34–57. Stoever defines Calvinism not as the teachings of Calvin but as that of the followers of Theodore Beza; see 177. In *Calvin and English*

Calvinism, R. T. Kendall, on the other hand, identifies Cotton's position as very close to that of Calvin; see 170–71, 182.

9. Sermon on Revelation 4:1–2, published by George Selement in "John Cotton's Hidden Antinomianism," *New England Historical and Genealogical Register* 129 (1975):288.

10. DeLamotte, "John Cotton and the Rhetoric of Grace," *Early American Literature* 21 (1986):65.

11. Winthrop, "Christian Charity," *Winthrop Papers* (Boston: Massachusetts Historical Society, 1929–1947), 2:294.

12. Winthrop, *Journal,* 1:195–96.

13. "The Elders Reply," in Hall, ed., *Antinomian Controversy,* 77.

14. Hall, *Antinomian Controversy,* 78.

15. "Mr. Cottons Revisall," quoted in Jesper Rosenmeier, "New England's Perfection: The Image of Adam and the Image of Christ in the Antinomian Controversy, 1634 to 1638," *William and Mary Quarterly,* 3d ser., 27 (1970):437.

16. Hooker, *The Soules Implantation* (London, 1637), 130.

17. *Journal,* 1:204.

18. Wheelwright, "A Fast-Day Sermon," in *Antinomian Controversy,* ed. Hall, 158.

19. *A Sermon . . . Deliver'd at Salem, 1636,* in *John Cotton on the Churches of New England,* ed. Larzer Ziff (Cambridge, Mass.: Harvard University Press, 1968), 62.

20. Winthrop, *Journal,* 1:211.

21. Recently much new information concerning Cotton's attitude toward Wheelwright has been published. See Sargent Bush, Jr., "'Revising what we have done amisse': John Cotton and John Wheelwright, 1640," *William and Mary Quarterly,* 3d ser., 45 (1988):734–50.

22. Stout, *The New England Soul: Preaching and Religious Culture in Colonial New England* (New York: Oxford University Press, 1986), 24–25.

23. Calvin, *Institutes,* vol. 3, chap. 2, sec. 7 and 29.

24. Miller, *The New England Mind: From Colony to Province* (Cambridge, Mass.: Harvard University Press, 1953), 62; Battis, *Saints and Sectaries,* 172.

25. Cotton Papers, Boston Public Library, part 2, no. 12.

26. *Bloudy Tenent, Washed,* part 2, 51.

27. *Magnalia Christi Americana,* 3:28.

28. Kendall, *Calvin and Calvinism,* 211.

Chapter Seven

1. This account of Williams's career is based on Ola E. Winslow, *Master Roger Williams* (New York: Macmillan, 1957).

2. "Moses His Judicialls," ed. Worthington C. Ford, *Proceedings of the Massachusetts Historical Society,* 2d ser., 16 (1903):281.

3. *A Letter of Mr. John Cottons* (London, 1643), 11.

4. *A Reply to Mr. Williams his Examination,* as published in *The Complete Writings of Roger Williams* (New York: Russell and Russell, 1963), 2:158–59.

5. Williams, *Mr. Cottons Letter Lately Printed,* in Williams, *Writings,* 1:331.

6. *Bloudy Tenent, Washed* (London, 1647), 48.

7. Williams, *Bloudy Tenent* (London, 1644), 43.

8. *The Controversie* (London, 1649), 7.

9. *Bloudy Tenent, Washed,* 126, 105. See also Sacvan Bercovitch, "Typology in Puritan New England: The Williams-Cotton Controversy Reassessed," *American Quarterly* 19 (1967):166–91.

10. Morgan, *Roger Williams: The Church and the State* (New York: Harcourt, Brace, World, 1967), 92. See also Jesper Rosenmeier, "The Teacher and the Witness: John Cotton and Roger Williams," *William and Mary Quarterly,* 3d ser., 25 (1968): 416–17 especially. Rosenmeier and Bercovitch have both shown that, though Cotton and Williams found little on which to agree, both read the Bible typologically.

11. Williams, *Mr. Cottons Letter Lately Printed,* in *Works,* 1:317.

12. *A Reply to Mr. Williams His Examination,* 7–8.

13. Morgan, *The Puritan Dilemma* (Boston: Little, Brown, 1958), 132.

Chapter Eight

1. Winthrop, *Journal* (New York: Scribner, 1908), 1:133 ff.

2. Norton, *Abel being Dead yet speaketh* (London, 1658), 22.

3. Miller, "Thomas Hooker and the Democracy of Early Connecticut," *New England Quarterly* 4 (1931):676.

4. Quoted from Thomas Hutchinson, *The History of Massachusetts Bay* (Cambridge, Mass.: Harvard University Press, 1936), 1:417; this text is quoted hereafter.

5. Winthrop, *Journal* (New York: Scribner, 1908), 1:151. The following account of *An Abstract, or The Lawes of New England* is indebted to Isabel Calder, "John Cotton's 'Moses His Judicials,'" *Publications of the Colonial Society of Massachusetts* 28 (1930–1933):86–94.

6. Theodore Dwight Bozeman, *To Live Ancient Lives: The Primitivist Dimension in Puritanism* (Chapel Hill: University of North Carolina Press, 1988), 175.

7. *Book of the General Laws,* ed. Thomas G. Barnes (San Marino, Calif.: Huntington Library, 1975), preface, and compare: Cotton to Winthrop, *Winthrop Papers* (Boston: Massachusetts Historical Society, 1929–1947), 5:193. For a discussion of church and state in Massachusetts, see David D. Hall, *The Faithful Shepherd: The New England Ministry in the Seventeenth Century* (Chapel Hill: University of North Carolina Press, 1972), chap. 6, and Edwin Powers, *Crime and Punishment in Early Massachusetts, 1620–1692: A Documentary History* (Boston: Beacon Press, 1966), 100–62; there Cotton's activities are explored.

8. Ford, "Cotton's 'Moses his Judicials,'" *Proceedings of the Massachusetts Historical Society,* 2d ser., 84. 16 (1903):274–78.

9. Winthrop, *Journal,* 1:124–25.

10. Ibid., 1:143–44.

11. *Records of the Governor and Company of the Massachusetts Bay in New England,* ed. Nathaniel B. Shurtleff (Boston: William White, 1853–1854), 1: 257–58.

12. Ibid., 1:157.

13. Darrett B. Rutman, *Winthrop's Boston: A Portrait of a Puritan Town, 1630–1649* (Chapel Hill: University of North Carolina Press, 1965), 79–81.

14. *Book of Lawes and Libertyes,* 53.

15. Bernard Bailyn, *The New England Merchants in the Seventeenth Century* (Cambridge, Mass.: Harvard University Press, 1955), 33.

16. A summary of Cotton's views appears in Winthrop's *Journal,* 1:317–18. See also *The Apologia of Robert Keayne: The Self-Portrait of a Puritan Merchant,* ed. Bernard Bailyn (New York: Harper and Row, 1965).

17. See James F. Stephen, *A History of the Criminal Law of England,* 3 vols. (London: Macmillan, 1883).

18. *Book of Lawes and Libertyes,* 6.

19. Calder, "Cotton's Moses," 94.

20. Haskins, *Law and Authority in Early Massachusetts* (New York: Macmillan, 1960), 126.

21. See Isabel M. Calder, "The Authorship of *A Discourse about Civil Government,*" *American Historical Review* 37 (1932):167–69, and Calder, "John Cotton and the New Haven Colony," *New England Quarterly* 3 (1930):82–94.

Chapter Nine

1. Jantz, *The First Century of New England Verse* (New York: Russell and Russell, 1962), 118–19. The best study of Puritan poetry does not consider Cotton's verses—Robert Daly, *God's Altar: The World and the Flesh in Puritan Poetry* (Berkeley: University of California Press, 1978).

2. Murdock, *Literature and Theology in Colonial New England* (Cambridge, Mass.: Harvard University Press, 1949), 143.

3. Cotton, preface to *The Whole Book of Psalmes* (Cambridge, Mass., 1640), sig.*³ [verso].

4. Jantz, *First Century,* 193.

5. See the Bibliography for sources of the texts of Cotton's poems.

Chapter Ten

1. See, for example, Larzer Ziff, "The Literary Consequences of Puritanism," in *The American Puritan Imagination: Essays in Revaluation,* ed. Sacvan Bercovitch (New York: Cambridge University Press, 1974).

2. Delbanco, *The Puritan Ordeal* (Cambridge, Mass.: Harvard University Press, 1989), 171.

3. Bozeman, *To Live Ancient Lives: The Primitivist Dimension in Puritanism* (Chapel Hill: University of North Carolina Press, 1988), 262.

4. Ziff, *The Career of John Cotton* (Princeton, N.J.: Princeton University Press, 1962), 160–61.

5. Boorstin, *The Americans: The Colonial Experience* (New York: Random House, 1958), 9.

6. *An Exposition upon The Thirteenth Chapter of the Revelation* (London, 1655), 72.

7. Murdock, *Literature and Theology in Colonial New England* (New York: Harper and Row, 1963), 189.

8. Nicholas R. Jones, "John Cotton," in *American Writers before 1800: A Biographical and Critical Dictionary* (Westport, Conn.: Greenwood Press, 1983), 1:392.

Selected Bibliography

PRIMARY SOURCES

The works of John Cotton are listed below in their order of composition, insofar as it can be determined. Dates of publication follow. The names of publishers for pre-1800 editions are omitted.

Works

1611 "A short discourse . . . touchinge the time when the Lordes day beginneth whether at the Eveninge or in the morninge. In Winton U. Solberg, "John Cotton's Treatise on the Duration of the Lord's Day." *Sibley's Heir, Publications of the Colonial Society of Massachusetts* 59 (1982):509–22.

1618 *Some Treasure Fetched out of Rubbish, or Three short but seasonable Treatises (found in a heap of scattered Papers).* [Only the first part is believed to be Cotton's.] London, 1660.

1620–1621 *A Brief Exposition Of the Whole Book of Canticles, or Song of Solomon.* London, 1642, 1648; Edinburgh: John Nichol, 1868.

1618–1625 *A Treatise of Mr. Cottons, Clearing certaine Doubts concerning Predestination. Together with an Examination Thereof: written by William Twisse, D.D.* London, 1646.

1622–1632 *Gods Mercie Mixed with his justice.* London, 1641: Facsimile reprint—Gainesville, Fla.: Scholars' Facsimiles and Reprints, 1958. Reprinted as *The Saints Support & Comfort.* London, 1658.

1624–1632 *Christ The Fountaine of Life; or Sundry Choyce Sermons on part of the fift Chapter of the first Epistle of St. John.* London, 1651 (twice). Facsimile reprint–New York: Arno Press, 1972.

1628 "Prefatory Epistle." In Arthur Hildersam, *Lectures upon the Fourth of John.* London, 1629.

1629–1632 *A Practical Commentary, or an Exposition with Observations, Reasons, and Uses upon The First Epistle Generall of John.* London, 1656, 1658. Reprinted as *An Exposition of First John.* Evansville, Ind.: Sovereign Grace Publishers, 1962.

1630   *Gods Promise to his Plantation . . . As it was delivered in a Sermon.* London, 1630, 1634, 1689; Boston: Old South Leaflets [1894].

1624–1632   *The way of Life, Or God's Way and Course, in bringing the Soule into; keeping it in, and carrying it on, in the wayes of life and peace.* London, 1641. Facsimile reprint–New York: AMS Press, 1983.

1634   *A Treatise I. Of Faith. II. Twelve Fundamental Articles of Christian Religion. III. Doctrinal Conclusion. IV. Questions and answers upon Church-Government.* [Boston,] 1713. Facsimile reprint–New York: AMS Press, 1983.

1635   *The True Constitution Of A particular visible Church, proved by Scripture.* London, 1642. Reprinted as *The Doctrine of the Church, To which is committed the Keyes of the Kingdome of Heaven.* London, 1643, 1644. Facsimile reprint–New York: Arno Press, 1972; New York: AMS Press, 1983.

1635   *The Controversie Concerning Liberty of Conscience in matters of Religion.* London, 1646, 1649. First published in Roger Williams, *The Bloudy Tenent of Persecution, for Cause of Conscience, Discussed.* London, 1644.

1636   "Answers" to "Certain Proposals made by Lord Say, Lord Brooke, and other Persons of quality, as conditions of their removing thereunto." In Thomas Hutchinson, *The History of . . . Massachusetts Bay.* London, 1764. Also in Thomas Hutchinson, *History,* edited by Lawrence S. Mayo. Cambridge, Mass.: Harvard University Press, 1936.

1636   "Copy of a Letter from Mr. Cotton to Lord Say and Seal." In Thomas Hutchinson, *The History of . . . Massachusetts Bay.* London, 1764. Also in Thomas Hutchinson, *History,* edited by Lawrence S. Mayo. Cambridge, Mass.: Harvard University Press, 1936. Also in *Letters from New England, 1629–1638: The Massachusetts Bay Colony,* edited by Everett Emerson. Amherst: University of Massachusetts Press, 1976.

1636   *A Letter of Mr. John Cottons . . . to Mr. Williams.* London, 1643.

1636   *A Sermon . . . Deliver'd at Salem.* Boston, 1713. In *John Cotton on the Churches of New England,* edited by Larzer Ziff. Cambridge, Mass.: Harvard University Press, 1968.

1636   *The New Covenant . . . Being the substance of sundry Sermons.* London, 1654. Reprinted as part of *The Covenant of Grace.* London, 1655. Reedited and published as *A Treatise of the Covenant of Grace.* London, 1659, 1671.

1636   *An Abstract, or The Lawes of New England, as they are now estab-*

lished. London, 1641. Reprinted with scriptural quotations as *An Abstract of Laws and Government*. London, 1655. Facsimile reprint—New York: AMS Press, 1983.

1636   *Sixteene Questions of Serious and Necessary Consequence*. London, 1644. Reprinted as *Severall Questions of Serious and Necessary Consequence*. London, 1647. Reprinted in *The Antinomian Controversy, 1636–1638: A Documentary History*, edited by David D. Hall. Middletown, Conn.: Wesleyan University Press, 1968.

1637   *A Coppy of A Letter of Mr. Cotton of Boston*. [London,] 1641. Reprinted in Emerson, *Letters from New England, 1629–1638: The Massachusetts Bay Colony*. Amherst: University of Massachusetts Press, 1976.

1637   *A Discourse about Civil Government in a New Plantation Whose Design is Religion*. Cambridge [Mass.], 1663.

1637   "Mr. Cottons Rejoynder." In *The Antinomian Controversy, 1636–1638: A Documentary History*, edited by David D. Hall. Middletown, Conn.: Wesleyan University Press, 1968.

1637   *A Conference Mr. John Cotton held at Boston*. London, 1646. Reprinted as *Gospel Conversion*. London, 1646. Reprinted with manuscript additions in *The Antinomian Controversy, 1636–1638: A Documentary History*, edited by David D. Hall. Middletown, Conn.: Wesleyan University Press, 1968.

1638   *A Modest and Cleare Answer to Mr. Balls Discourse of set formes of Prayer*. London, 1642 (twice).

1638–1639   "Sermon on Revelation 4:1–2." Published by George Selement in "John Cotton's Hidden Antinomianism." *New England Historical and Genealogical Register* 129 (1975):283–94.

1639–1640   *An Exposition upon The Thirteenth Chapter of the Revelation*. London, 1655, 1656. Facsimile reprint–New York: Arno Press, 1982.

1641   *The Powrring out of the Seven Vials: or, An Exposition of the Sixteenth Chapter of the Revelation, with an Application of it to our Times*. London, 1642, 1645.

1641   *The Churches Resurrection*. London, 1642. Facsimile reprint–New York: Arno Press, 1982.

1641   *A Brief Exposition With Practical Observations Upon the Whole Book of Canticles. Never before Printed*. London, 1655. Facsimile reprint–New York: Arno Press, 1972.

1641   *The Way of the Churches of Christ in New-England*. London, 1645. Facsimile reprint–New York: AMS Press, 1983.

1643   *The Keyes of the Kingdom of Heaven*. London, 1644 (six times); Boston: Tappan and Dennet, 1843. Reprinted in *John Cotton on the Churches of New England,* edited by Larzer Ziff. Cambridge, Mass.: Harvard University Press, 1968.

1643   *The Grounds and Ends of the Baptisme of the Children of the Faithfull.* London, 1647.

1644   *A Briefe Exposition with Practical Observations upon the Whole Book of Ecclesiastes.* London, 1654, 1657; Edinburgh: John Nichol, 1868.

1644   *The Covenant of Gods Free Grace.* London, 1645. Facsimile reprint– New York: AMS Press, 1983.

1645   *A Reply to Mr. Williams His Examination.* London, 1647. Bound with Cotton's *The Bloudy Tenent, Washed,* but separate from it in content and pagination. Reprinted in *The Complete Writings of Roger Williams.* New York: Russell and Russell, 1963, vol. 2.

1645   *Milk for Babes. Drawn Out of the Breasts of both Testaments.* London, 1646, 1648; Boston, 1656; London, 1668, 1672; Cambridge, Mass., 1691; Boston, 1720, 1747.

1646   *The Bloudy Tenent, Washed and Made White in the Bloud of the Lambe.* London, 1647. Reprinted in *The Complete Writings of Roger Williams.* New York: Russell and Russell, 1963, vol. 3. Facsimile reprint–New York: Arno Press, 1972.

1646   *Singing of Psalmes a Gospel Ordinance.* London, 1647, 1650.

1647   "Prefatory Epistle." In John Norton, *Responsio ad totam questionum syllogen à Guilemo Apollonio propositam.* London, 1648. Republished in English as *The Answer to the Whole Set of Questions of the Celebrated Mr. William Apollonius.* Cambridge, Mass.: Harvard University Press, 1958.

1647   *The Way of Congregational Churches Cleared.* London, 1648.

1649   *Of the Holinesse of Church Members.* London, 1650.

1651   *A Defence of Mr. John Cotton From the Imputation of Selfe Contradiction.* Oxford, 1658.

1651   *Certain Queries Tending to Accommodation, and Communion of Presbyterian and Congregational Churches.* London, 1654.

1651   "Prefatory Epistle." In John Norton, *The Orthodox Evangelist.* London, 1654.

1651   "Sermon upon a Day of Publique thanksgiving." Published by Francis J. Bremer in *William and Mary Quarterly,* 3d ser., 37 (1980):110–24.

Personal Letters

Some of Cotton's letters have been published; a few are cited in the notes. An edition of Cotton's complete extant correspondence is being prepared by Professor Sargent Bush. A census of Cotton letters appears in *Early American Literature* 24 (1989):91–111.

Published Poems

ca. 1610   "Lines describing an extreme Puritan" (a fragment). Quoted in William Coddington, *A Demonstration of True Love unto the Rulers of the Massachusetts.* N.p., 1674, 20.

1633   "Another poem . . . upon his removal from Boston to this Wilderness." Published in John Norton, *Abel being Dead yet Liveth.* London, 1658, 29–30.

1647   "On my Reverend and dear Brother Mr. Thomas Hooker." Published in Thomas Hooker, *A Survey of the Summe of Church-Discipline.* London, 1648, preface.

1649   "In Saram," "In Rolandum," "In Utrumque." Published in Cotton Mather, *Magnalia Christi Americana.* London, 1702, and subsequent editions.

1651   "To my Reverend Brother Mr. Samuel Stone, Teacher of the Church at Hartford." Published in Samuel Stone, *A Congregational Church Is a Catholike Visible Church.* London, 1652, preface.

1652   "A thankful Acknowledgment of God's Providence." Published in Norton, *Abel,* 28–29.

SECONDARY SOURCES

Books and Parts of Books

Bozeman, Theodore Dwight. *To Live Ancient Lives: The Primitivist Dimension of Puritanism.* Chapel Hill: University of North Carolina Press, 1988. Describes Puritanism as an attempt to return to primitive Christianity. Cotton provides the words of the title and is the subject of a chapter.

Cohen, Charles Lloyd. *God's Caress: The Psychology of Puritan Religious Experience.* New York: Oxford University Press, 1986. Examines Cotton's notions of religious conversion and their Puritan context. A fresh, important, precise, and demanding study.

Delbanco, Andrew. *The Puritan Ordeal.* Cambridge, Mass.: Harvard University

Press, 1989. A study of the development of Puritanism in America till about 1650 and its English background. Cotton is a major figure in the book.

Gura, Philip F. *A Glimpse of Sion's Glory: Puritan Radicalism in New England, 1620–1660.* Wesleyan, Conn.: Wesleyan University Press, 1984. A superb study of antinomianism and other deviations from mainstream Puritanism, with Cotton a central figure.

Hall, David D. *The Faithful Shepherd: A History of the New England Ministry in the Seventeenth Century.* Chapel Hill: University of North Carolina Press, 1972. Explores with precision the place of John Cotton in the development of American Puritanism.

————, ed. *The Antinomian Controversy, 1636–1638: A Documentary History.* Middletown, Conn.: Wesleyan University Press, 1968. Provides the major documents for an understanding of the controversy and helpful explanatory materials. Besides selections from Cotton's writings about the controversy, includes the first publication of Cotton's substantial "Rejoynder," described by Hall as "the most important exposition of Cotton's theology at the time of the Controversy."

Hambrick-Stowe, Charles E. *The Practice of Piety: Puritan Devotional Disciplines in Seventeenth-Century New England.* Chapel Hill: University of North Carolina Press, 1982. An outstanding study of Puritanism, with much information about Cotton's notions of prayer, the use of psalms, and related matters.

Holifield, E. Brooks. *The Covenant Sealed: The Development of Puritan Sacramental Theology in Old and New England, 1570–1720.* New Haven, Conn.: Yale University Press, 1974. Provides a full context for Cotton's views on baptism and the Lord's Supper.

Kendall, R. T. *Calvinism and English Calvinism to 1649.* Oxford: Oxford University Press, 1979. Places the theology of Cotton, the subject of a chapter, in the context of Calvinism.

Kibbey, Ann. *The Interpretation of Material Shapes in Puritanism: A Study of Rhetoric, Prejudice, and Violence.* Cambridge, England: Cambridge University Press, 1986. As suggested by the subtitle, Kibbey examines the social and artistic values of Puritanism; Cotton is the central figure of the book.

Lowance, Mason I., Jr. *The Language of Canaan: Metaphor and Symbol in New England from the Puritans to the Transcendentalists.* Cambridge, Mass.: Harvard University Press, 1980. Provides a context for Cotton's typological thought.

Mather, Cotton. *Magnalia Christi Americana.* London, 1702. Contains a biography of Cotton and information about the events of his life in Massachusetts.

Norton, John. *Abel being Dead yet speaketh: or, The Life & Death of . . . Mr. John Cotton.* London, 1658.

Pettit, Norman. *The Heart Prepared: Grace and Conversion in Puritan Spiritual Life.* 2d ed. Middletown, Conn.: Wesleyan University Press, 1989. Provides an intelligent and readable account of Cotton's role in the Antinomian Controversy.

Rutman, Darrett B. *Winthrop's Boston: A Portrait of a Puritan Town, 1630–1649.* Chapel Hill: University of North Carolina Press, 1965. Provides a context for Cotton's experiences and work in Boston, Massachusetts.

Stoever, William K. B. *"A Faire and Easie Way to Heaven": Covenant Theology and Antinomianism in Early Massachusetts.* Middletown, Conn.: Wesleyan University Press, 1978. The fullest study of the theological issues in the Antinomian Controversy. Cotton is a central figure in the book.

Toulouse, Teresa. *The Art of Prophesying: New England Sermons and the Shaping of Belief.* Athens: University of Georgia Press, 1987. Includes an important chapter on Cotton's preaching.

Whiting, Samuel. "Concerning the Life of the Famous Mr. Cotton, Teacher to the Church of Christ at Boston, in New-England." In *Chronicles of the First Planters of the Colony of Massachusetts Bay, from 1623 to 1636,* edited by Alexander Young. Boston: Charles C. Little and James Brown, 1846. Norton used this brief biography by Whiting, who was a Massachusetts minister and contemporary of Cotton.

Ziff, Larzer. *The Career of John Cotton: Puritanism and the American Experience.* Princeton, N.J.: Princeton University Press, 1962. An excellent biographical study.

Journal Articles

Bercovitch, Sacvan. "Typology in Puritan New England: The Williams-Cotton Controversy Reassessed." *American Quarterly* 19 (1967):166–91. Emphasizes Cotton's dedication to typology.

Bremer, Francis J. "In Defense of Regicide: John Cotton on the Execution of Charles I." *William and Mary Quarterly,* 3d ser., 37 (1980):103–24. Reproduces a sermon by Cotton.

DeLamotte, Eugenia. "John Cotton and the Rhetoric of Grace." *Early American Literature* 21 (1986):49–74. A major article that examines the special character of Cotton's sermons.

Grabo, Norman S. "John Cotton's Aesthetics: A Sketch." *Early American Literature* 3 (Spring 1968):3–10. A brief but insightful essay.

Rosenmeier, Jesper. "New England's Perfection: The Image of Adam and the Image of Christ in the Antinomian Controversy." *William and Mary Quarterly,* 3d ser., 27 (1970):435–59. A valuable analysis of Cotton's differences from the other Puritan ministers.

————. "'Clearing the Medium': A Reevaluation of John Cotton's *A Practicall Commentary Upon the First Epistle Generall of John.*" *William and Mary Quarterly,* 3d ser., 37 (1980):577–91. Examines the relationship of Cotton's theology to his rhetoric.

Selement, George. "John Cotton's Hidden Antinomianism: His Sermon on

Revelation 4:1–2." *New England Historical and Genealogical Register* 129 (1975):278–94. Reproduces a 1639 sermon as recorded by Thomas Shepard.

Solberg, Winton U. "John Cotton's Treatise on the Duration of the Lord's Day." *Sibley's Heir, Publications of the Colonial Society of Massachusetts* 59 (1982):505–22.

Background Reading

The literature on Puritanism is enormous and much of it excellent. The baker's dozen items below provide an introduction.

Bercovitch, Sacvan. *The Puritan Origins of the American Self.* New Haven, Conn.: Yale University Press, 1975. A brilliant and wide-ranging study, centering on John Cotton's grandson and his biography of John Winthrop.

Emerson, Everett. *English Puritanism from John Hooper to John Milton.* Durham, N.C.: Duke University Press, 1968. Provides a historical overview of Cotton's English background and samples of the writings of many Puritans.

———, ed. *Letters from New England: The Massachusetts Bay Colony, 1629–1638.* Amherst: University of Massachusetts Press, 1976. The story of the Puritan colony's beginnings, told by means of fifty-six letters, including four by John Cotton.

———. *Puritanism in America, 1620–1750.* Boston: G. K. Hall, 1977. Provides a concise description of New England Puritanism.

Hall, David D. *Worlds of Wonder, Days of Judgment: Popular Religious Belief in Early New England.* New York: Knopf, 1989. A fresh and original examination of the popular religion that was underneath Puritanism.

Heimert, Alan, and Andrew Delbanco, eds. *The Puritans in America: A Narrative Anthology.* Cambridge, Mass.: Harvard University Press, 1985. Provides valuable bibliographies in conjunction with its selections.

Holifield, E. Brooks. *Era of Persuasion: American Thought and Culture, 1521–1680.* Boston: G. K. Hall, 1989. An excellent portrait of Puritanism in its American context.

Middlekauf, Robert. *The Mathers: Three Generations of Puritan Intellectuals.* New York: Oxford University Press, 1971. Focuses on Richard, Increase, and Cotton Mather but sees their careers in a broad context. Readable.

Miller, Perry. *Orthodoxy in Massachusetts, 1630–1650.* Cambridge, Mass.: Harvard University Press, 1933. A study of the origins of congregationalism.

———. *The New England Mind: The Seventeenth Century.* New York: Macmillan, 1939. The fundamental study, often criticized but still a monument.

Morgan, Edmund S. *The Puritan Dilemma: The Story of John Winthrop.* Boston: Little, Brown, 1958. An outstanding account of Cotton's parishioner and the governor of the Massachusetts Bay Colony.

Stout, Harry. *The New England Soul: Preaching and Religious Culture in Colonial*

New England. New York: Oxford University Press, 1986. A full and detailed examination of the New England sermon.

Ziff, Larzer. *Puritanism in America: New Culture in a New World.* New York: Viking, 1973. An engaging account, learned and insightful, of Puritanism.

Index

Adams, Thomas, 15
Allen, Thomas, 15
Ames, William, 3, 21, 52, 53, 56, 76, 102, 124
Anabapists, 8
Andrewes, Lancelot, 14
Antinomian Controversy, 29, 42, 51, 64, 66, 85–96, 107, 123, 124
Apollonius, William, 56
Aquinas, Thomas, 3
Aristotle, 3
Arminianism, 6
Ash, Simeon, 44
Augustine, 56, 67, 80, 84, 120

Baillie, Robert, 51, 60, 86
Ball, John, 10
Baptism, 8–9
Baptists, 51
Barrow, Henry, 51
Battis, Emory, 92, 95
Baynes, Paul, 26, 52, 56
Bellarmine, Robert, 3
Bellingham, Richard, 112
Beza, Theodore, 3, 6, 66, 81, 84
Boorstin, Daniel, 124
Boston (Lincolnshire), 3, 10, 60, 120, 123, 124
Boston (Mass.), 4, 10, 16, 37, 41, 87, 94, 95, 103, 123, 125
Bozeman, Theodore Dwight, 21, 72, 124
Bradshaw, William, 52
Bradstreet, Anne, 119
Brightman, Thomas, 21
Browne, Robert, 51
Brownists, 8, 44
Bucer, Martin, 80
Bullinger, Heinrich, 80

Calder, Isabel M., 117
Calvin, John, 3, 5, 6, 21, 32, 66, 67, 80–81, 82, 90, 94, 102, 124

Calvinism, 3, 6, 29, 64, 66, 67, 88, 93, 96, 102
Cambridge Platform, 56–59
Cambridge University, 1–3, 4, 6, 7, 15, 80
Capitalism, 26
Cartwright, Thomas, 3, 6, 51
Cawdrey, Daniel, 55, 62
Chaderton, Thomas, 2, 6
Charles I, 38, 39, 79
Clarke, Samuel, 2
Clinton, Theophilus, Earl of Lincoln, 9
Come, Donald, 119
Congregationalism, 8, 22, 35–62, 75
Copernicus, 70
Cotton, John

LIFE
Education, 2–4, 6–7; at St. Botolph's Church, 3–4, 8–9, 16, 36, 37, 39, 59, 86, 124; in Boston, Massachusetts, 4, 10, 36, 87–89, 96

WORKS
"Answers" to "Certain Proposals made by Lord Say, Lord Brooke, and other Persons of quality," 111–112
Abstract; or The Lawes of New England, An, 112–117
Bloudy Tenent, Washed, The, 62, 86, 105, 109, 125
Brief Exposition Of the Whole Book of Canticles, A, 20–23, 67
Brief Exposition With Practical Observations Upon the Whole Book of Canticles, A, 67–69
Briefe Exposition with Practical Observations upon the Whole Book of Ecclesiastes, A, 69–71
Certain Queries Tending to Accommodation, 61–62
Christ The Fountaine of Life, 29–33
Churches Resurrection, The, 72, 77

Conference Mr. John Cotton held at Boston, A, 86, 94–96

Controversie Concerning Liberty of Conscience, The, 105

Coppy of a Letter, A, 44–45, 48

"Copy of a Letter to Lord Say and Seal," 43–44, 111, 125

Covenant of Gods Free Grace, The, 77–78

Covenant of Grace, The, 61, 63

Defence of Mr. John Cotton, A, 62

Discourse about Civil Government, A, 117–118

Exposition upon The Thirteenth Chapter of the Revelation, 71–75

Gods Mercie Mixed with his justice, 17–20, 125

Gods Promise to his Plantation, 33–34

Gospel Conversion, 86, 94–96

Grounds and Ends of the Baptisme of the Children, The, 8–9

"How Far Moses Judicialls Bind Massachusetts," 113

Letter of Mr. John Cottons . . . to Mr. Williams, A, 105

Keyes of the Kingdom of Heaven, The, 45, 48–50, 58, 62

Milk for Babes, 96–102, 125

"Mr. Cottons Rejoynder," 90–91

"Mr. Cotton's Revisall," 91

Modest and Cleare Answer to Mr. Balls Discourse of set formes of Prayer, A, 10–11

New Covenant, The, 63

Of the Holinesse of Church Members, 60–61, 79

Powring out of the Seven Vials, The, 71–72, 75–76, 125

Practical Commentary . . . upon The First Epistle Generall of John, A, 27–29

"Preface" to *The Whole Book of Psalmes Faithfully Translated into English Meter,* 12

"Prefatory Epistle" to John Norton, *Responsio,* 56

"Prefatory Epistle" to John Norton, *The Orthodox Evangelist,* 10

"Prefatory Epistle" to Arthur Hildersam, *Lectures upon the Fourth of John,* 16–17

Reply to Mr. Williams His Examination, A, 86, 96, 105

Sermon . . . Deliver'd at Salem, 41–43, 91–92

"Sermon on Revelation 4:1–2," 88

"Sermon upon a Day of Publique thanksgiving," 79

Severall Questions of Serious and Necessary Consequence, 86, 89–94

"Short discourse . . . touchinge the time when the Lordes day beginneth, A," 7

Singing of Psalmes a Gospel Ordinance, 11, 119

Sixteene Questions of Serious and Necessary Consequence, 86, 89–94

Some Treasure Fetched out Rubbish, 7

Treatise I. Of Faith, A, 84–85

Treatise of Mr. Cottons, Clearing certaine Doubts concerning Predestination, A, 83–84

Treatise of the Covenant of Grace, A, 31, 63–67, 87

True Constitution Of A particular visible Church, The, 40–41

way of Life, The, 23–27

Way of Congregational Churches Cleared, The, 51–56, 62, 86, 91, 92, 93, 94, 95, 96, 125

Way of the Churches of Christ in New-England, The, 45–48

Covenant theology, 8–9, 30, 41–43, 64–67, 78, 90

Cromwell, Oliver, 39, 77

Davenport, John, 10, 44, 48, 53, 117

DeLamotte, Eugenia, 2, 18, 88

Delbanco, Andrew, 123

Dent, Arthur, 8

Dod, John, 2

Donne, John, 14

Dudley, Thomas, 112

Edward VI, 76

Edwards, Thomas, 49
Eliot, John, 53
Elizabeth I, 5, 13
Emerson, Ralph Waldo, 12, 123, 124, 125
Emmanuel College, Cambridge University, 2, 3, 6, 15
England, Church of, 6, 8, 9, 13, 23, 28, 35, 36, 39, 47, 51, 54, 103, 104
Episcopacy, 39

Familism, 51, 88, 96
Fiske, John, 119
Ford, Worthington C., 113
Franklin, Benjamin, 123
Fuller, Samuel, 41
Fuller, Thomas, 81

Gataker, Thomas, 2, 28
Gilby, Anthony, 8
Goodwin, Thomas, 2, 48, 56
Gouge, William, 2

Habegger, Alfred, 18
Haller, William, 13, 38
Hammond, Jeffrey, 68
Hampton Court Conference, 6
Haraszti, Zoltan, 12
Harris, Robert, 2, 14
Harvard College, 2
Haskins, George, 117
Hawthorne, Nathaniel, 12, 123
Haynes, John, 112
Henry VIII, 5, 76
Heppe, Heinrich, 31
Hibbins, Anne, 61
Hildersam, Arthur, 2, 16
Hooker, Richard, 80
Hooker, Thomas, 2, 10, 13, 23, 25, 31, 45–46, 48, 52, 54, 56, 62, 65, 91, 104, 119, 120, 121, 125, 126
Horton, Douglas, 56
Hutchinson, Anne, 4, 38, 42, 51, 64, 66, 85–90, 91, 92–96, 124
Hutchinson, Thomas, 43

Independents, 39, 51
Indians. See Native Americans

James I, 5, 6, 51
Jantz, Harold, 119
Jewel, John, 3
Johnson, Edward, 126
Junius, 3, 56, 76

Keayne, Robert, 46, 115

Lathrop, John, 37
Laud, William, 38
Levy, Babette, 2
Luther, Martin, 21

Maclear, J. F., 72
Martyr, Peter, 3, 84
Mary I, 5, 33, 76, 80
Massachusetts Bay Colony, 4, 35, 44, 52, 85, 102, 103, 110, 118, 119, 124, 126
Mather, Cotton, 1, 3, 4, 102, 121
Mather, Richard, 57
Miller, Perry, 45, 53, 95, 110
Millennium, 33, 69, 72, 77
Milton, John, 77
Morgan, Edmund S., 43, 78, 108, 109
Murdock, Kenneth B., 119, 125

Native Americans, 33, 34, 53
New Haven, 117
Norton, John, 3, 10, 16, 56, 110
Nowell, Alexander, 80
Nye, Philip, 48, 56

Organicism, 1, *106–109*, 114, 118
Owen, John, 62
Oxford University, 80

Quakers, 88
Queen's College, Cambridge University, 15–16

Parker, Robert, 52
Paraeus, 84
Partridge, Ralph, 57
Perkins, William, 1, 3, 17, 66, 76, 82, 83, 84, 102
Peter, Hugh, 52, 79, 112
Piscator, 3

Plymouth (Mass.), 41, 103, 104, 125
Preaching, *13–16,* 17, 63
Presbyterianism, 5, 6, 38, 39, 50, 51, 54, 57, 58, 59, 60, 61, 62, 79
Preston, John, 2, 15, 27
Puritanism, *5–12* and passim

Ramus, Peter, 3
Rathband, William, 44
Rhode Island, 104
Robinson, John, 51
Rogers, Nathaniel, 119
Roman Catholicism, 5, 8, 25, 72, 73, 74, 75, 76
Rutherford, Samuel, 55, 60
Rutman, Darrett, 78

St. Botolph's Church, 3, 4, 7, 8, 9, 36, 120, 124
Salem (Mass.), 36, 37, 41–43, 50, 91, 93, 103, 104, 109, 119
Say and Seal, Lord, 43–44, 48, 111, 125
Seekers, 51, 106
Separatism, 8, 22, 28, 36, 41, 44, 51
Sharpe, Samuel, 119
Shepard, Thomas, 2, 11, 23, 54, 112, 123, 126
Sibbes, Richard, 1, 14, 15, 20, 124
Simpson, Sidrach, 56
Skelton, Samuel, 41
Smith, Henry, 14
Some, Robert, 15
Southampton (Long Island), 117
Stearns, Raymond P., 38
Stoddard, Solomon, 47
Stone, Samuel, 95, 121

Stout, Harry S., 93
Swallowe, Matthias, 17, 20

Talmud, 21
Targum, 21
Tawney, Richard H., 26
Taylor, Edward, 119
Toulouse, Teresa, 2, 18, 19
Twisse, William, 83, 94, 96
Tyler, Moses Coit, 2
Typology, 21–22

Udall, John, 6, 8

Vane, Sir Henry, 89, 91, 92, 111, 112

Walker, Williston, 58
Ward, Samuel, 9
Weber, Max, 29
Westminster Assembly, 38, 39, 48, 51, 57
Westminster Confession, 23, 58
Wheelwright, John, 86, 91–92
Whitaker, William, 3, 56, 76
Whitgift, John, 3
Williams, John, 9
Williams, Roger, 11, 38, 41, 44, 51, 86, *103–109,* 124
Wilson, John, 1, 61, 63, 78, 87, 88, 91, 119
Winthrop, John, 4, 33, 35, 36, 44, 79, 86, 89, 92, 103, 109, 110, 112, 123
Woodbridge, Benjamin, 8, 63

Zanchius, 3, 84
Ziff, Larzer, 2, 47, 65, 124

DEMCO